The Swedish Americans

THE IMMIGRANT EXPERIENCE

The Swedish Americans

Allyson McGill

Sandra Stotsky, General Editor
Harvard University Graduate School of Education

CHELSEA HOUSE PUBLISHERS

Philadelphia

CHELSEA HOUSE PUBLISHERS
Editorial Director: Richard Rennert
Production Manager: Pamela Loos
Art Director: Sara Davis
Picture Editors: Judy Hasday, Adrian Allen
Senior Production Editor: Lisa Chippendale

Staff for THE SWEDISH AMERICANS
Editors: Petra Press and Reed Ueda
Designer: Noreen M. Lamb
Cover Illustrator: Jane Sterrett

3 5 7 9 8 6 4 2

Library of Congress Cataloging-in-Publication Data

McGill, Allyson.
    The Swedish Americans/Allyson McGill.
    p. cm. — (The immigrant experience)
    Includes bibliographical references and index.
    ISBN 0-7910-4551-X (hardcover: alk. paper).
    ISBN 0-7910-4552-8 (pbk.: alk. paper).
    1. Swedish Americans—Juvenile literature. I. Title.
    II. Series.
E184.S23M47 1997
973'.04397—dc21   96-36783
                                                   CIP
                                                   AC

CONTENTS

THE IMMIGRANT EXPERIENCE

CHELSEA HOUSE PUBLISHERS

A
NATION
OF
NATIONS

Daniel Patrick Moynihan

The Constitution of the United States begins: "We the People of the United States…" Yet, as we know, the United States was not then and is not now made up of a single group of people. It is made up of many peoples. Immigrants and bondsmen from Europe, Asia, Africa, and Central and South America came here or were brought here, and still they come. They forged one nation and made it their own. More than 100 years ago, Walt Whitman expressed this great central fact of America: "Here is not merely a nation, but a teeming Nation of nations."

Although the ingenuity and acts of courage of these immigrants, our ancestors, shaped the North American way of life, we sometimes take their contributions for granted. This fine series, *The Immigrant Experience,* examines the experiences and contributions of different immigrant groups and how these contributions determined the future of the United States and Canada.

Immigrants did not abandon their ethnic traditions when they reached the shores of North America. Each ethnic group had its own customs and traditions, and each brought different experiences, accomplishments, skills, values, styles of dress, and tastes in food that lingered long after its arrival. Yet this profusion of differences created a singularity, or bond, among the immigrants.

The United States and Canada are unusual in this respect. Whereas religious and ethnic differences have sparked intolerance throughout the rest of the world—from the 17th-century religious wars to the 19th-century nationalist movements in Europe to the near extermination of the Jewish people under Nazi Germany— North Americans have struggled to learn how to respect each other's differences and live in harmony.

Our two countries are hardly the only two in which different groups must learn to live together. There is no nation of significant size anywhere in the world which would not be classified as multi-ethnic. But only in North America are there so *many* different groups, most of them living cheek by jowl with one another.

This is not easy. Look around the world. And it has not always been easy for us. Witness the exclusion of Chinese immigrants, and for practical purposes Japanese also, in the late 19th century. But by the late 20th century, Chinese and Japanese Americans were the most successful of all the groups recorded by the census. We have had prejudice aplenty, but it has been resisted and recurrently overcome.

The remarkable ability of Americans to live together as one people was seriously threatened by the issue of slavery. Thousands of settlers from the British Isles had arrived in the colonies as indentured servants, agreeing to work for a specified number of years on farms or as apprentices in return for passage to America and room and board. When the first Africans arrived in the then-British colonies during the 17th century, some colonists thought that they too should be treated as indentured servants. Eventually, the question of whether the Africans should be treated as inden-tured, like the English, or as slaves who could be owned for life was considered in a Maryland court. The court's calamitous decree held that blacks were slaves bound to a lifelong servitude, and so also were their children. America went through a time of moral ex-amination and civil war before it finally freed African slaves and their descendants. The principle that all people are created equal had faced its greatest challenge and survived.

Yet the court ruling that set blacks apart from other races fanned flames of discrimination that burned long after slavery was abolished—and that still flicker today. Indeed, it was about the time of the American Civil War that European theories of evolution were turned to the service of ranking different peoples by their presumed distance from our apelike ancestors.

When the Irish flooded American cities to escape the famine in Ireland, the cartoonists caricatured the typical "Paddy" (a common term for Irish immigrants) as an apelike creature with jutting jaw and sloping forehead.

By the 20th century, racism and ethnic prejudice had given rise to virulent theories of a Northern European master race. When Adolf Hitler came to power in Germany in 1933, he popularized the notion of an Aryan race. Only a man of the deepest ignorance and evil could have done this. *Aryan* is a Sanskrit word, which is to say the ancient script of what we now think of as India. It means "noble" and was adopted by linguists—notably by a fine German scholar, Max Müller—to denote the Indo-European family of languages. Müller was horrified that anyone could think of it in terms of race, especially a race of blond-haired, blue-eyed Teutons. But the Nazis embraced the notion of a master race. Anyone with darker and heavier features was considered inferior. Buttressed by these theories, the German Nazi state from 1933 to 1945 set out to destroy European Jews, along with Poles, Gypsies, Russians, and other groups considered inferior. It nearly succeeded. Millions of these people were murdered.

The tragedies brought on by ethnic and racial intolerance throughout the world demonstrate the importance of North America's efforts to create a society free of prejudice and inequality.

A relatively recent example of the New World's desire to resolve ethnic friction nonviolently is the solution that the Canadians found to a conflict between two ethnic groups. A long-standing dispute as to whether Canadian culture was properly English or French resurfaced in the mid-1960s, dividing the peoples of the French-speaking Province of Quebec from those of the English-speaking provinces. Relations grew tense, then bitter, then violent. The Royal Commission on Bilingualism and Biculturalism was established to study the growing crisis and to propose measures to ease the tensions. As a result of the commission's recommendations, all official documents and statements from the national government's capital at Ottawa are now issued in both French and English, and bilingual education is encouraged.

The year 1980 marked a coming of age for the United States's ethnic heritage. For the first time, the U.S. Bureau of the Census asked people about their ethnic background. Americans chose from more than 100 groups, including French Basque, Spanish Basque, French Canadian, African-American, Peruvian, Armenian, Chinese, and Japanese. The ethnic group with the largest response was English (49.6 million). More than 100 million Americans claimed ancestors from the British Isles, which includes England, Ireland, Wales, and Scotland. There were almost as many Germans (49.2 million) as English. The Irish-American population (40.2 million) was third, but the next-largest ethnic group, the African-Americans, was a distant fourth (21 million). There was a sizable group of French ancestry (13 million) as well as of Italian (12 million). Poles, Dutch, Swedes, Norwegians, and Russians followed. These groups, and other smaller ones, represent the wondrous profusion of ethnic influences in North America.

Canada too has learned more about the diversity of its population. Studies conducted during the French/English conflict showed that Canadians were descended from Ukrainians, Germans, Italians, Chinese, Japanese, native Indians, and Inuit, among others. Canada found it had no ethnic majority, although nearly half of its immigrant population had come from the British Isles. Canada, like the United States, is a land of immigrants for whom mutual tolerance is a matter of reason as well as principle. But note how difficult this can be in practice, even for persons of manifest goodwill.

The people of North America are the descendants of one of the greatest migrations in history. And that migration is not over.

Koreans, Vietnamese, Nicaraguans, Cubans, and many others are heading for the shores of North America in large numbers. This mix of cultures shapes every aspect of our lives. To understand ourselves, we must know something about our diverse ethnic ancestry. Nothing so defines the North American nations as the motto on the Great Seal of the United States: *E Pluribus Unum*—Out of Many, One.

In 1782, Sweden's king Gustav III (at right) recognized the newly formed American republic.

PIONEERS

In the spring of 1782, Sweden's King Gustav III learned that Britain had just surrendered to rebel forces in colonial America. Gustav immediately dispatched an envoy to Paris with instructions for the Swedish ambassador, who was ordered to meet with the American envoy in Paris, Benjamin Franklin, and negotiate a treaty. Designed to encourage friendship and trade between the United States and Sweden, the treaty conferred instant legitimacy on the newborn nation. Many Americans shared the gratitude expressed by one of the country's founders, John Adams, when he wrote later that year, "Tell [the ambassador from Sweden] privately that we shall see to it that we remember that it was his sovereign who was the first to do us this honor."

In the following century the United States would owe an even greater debt to Sweden. For Swedish immigrants, more than those from any other nation, were responsible for taming the wilderness of America's vast territories in the Midwest and Pacific Northwest. These immigrants arrived with skills that figured crucially in America's push westward. They were adept at logging, farming, mining, fishing, and construction. As pioneering settlers, Swedish Americans truly helped expand the nation's breadth "from sea to shining sea."

Although some Swedish immigrants had arrived on America's shores as early as the 1600s, most did not arrive until the second half of the 19th century. This wave of newcomers, however, was truly enormous: Between 1851 and 1930, 1.2 million Swedes left their native land to seek a better life in America. Only Ireland, Norway, and possibly Iceland have lost a higher percentage of their people to the New World. So many came because America offered abundant space and employment, advantages their native country could no longer provide.

It nevertheless took great courage for Swedes to pack up all their possessions and leave behind everything they knew. They had to travel across a wide ocean, weathering storms that threatened to destroy their ships long before they ever reached the faraway port of New York. And once they stepped ashore, after a voyage that lasted months, they found themselves in a country where they seldom knew anyone and where an alien language was spoken.

Entire families—husbands, wives, and children, often grandparents, cousins, aunts, and uncles—departed for the New World knowing that they might never again set eyes on their native land or their kin. One emigrant daughter wrote to her parents in Sweden:

> You write that you miss me very much. That is not to be wondered at, because nothing lies closer to the heart than the love between children and parents. But, pray, do not worry too much about me. I got along well in Sweden, and this being a better country, I will do even better here. As my plans are now, I have no desire to be in Sweden. I never expect to speak with you again in this life. . . . Your loving daughter unto death, Mary Jonson.

Although the enormous masses of Swedish immigrants stopped arriving in America in 1939, a large Swedish-American presence remains. According to the 1990 U.S. census, 4,680,863 citizens reported

Swedish ancestry. Of that number, almost 30 percent claimed they were of exclusively Swedish descent, a very high percentage considering that emigration essentially halted almost 70 years ago.

Because the land was the great lure, many Swedish Americans still live in the regions settled by their forebears. Over 50 percent live in the Western states of California, Washington, and Hawaii or the Midwestern states of Minnesota, Illinois, Wisconsin, Ohio, and Indiana. California, with a population of 590,000, and Minnesota, with 535,000, contain by far the largest concentrations of Swedish Americans. A substantial number have ventured into other regions of the United States over the years as well, and today, people of Swedish American descent inhabit every state in the United States and every province in Canada.

The men and women who courageously risked their futures for the chance of a more promising life in America expected much of the New World, sometimes too much. Nonetheless, they coped with the sometimes grueling realities of the immigrant experience and went on to enrich their new homeland. A legacy of contribution links the pioneers who helped settle the American frontier to their descendants who excel today in politics, science, business, and the arts. Swedish Americans have returned as much to North America as the continent gave to them.

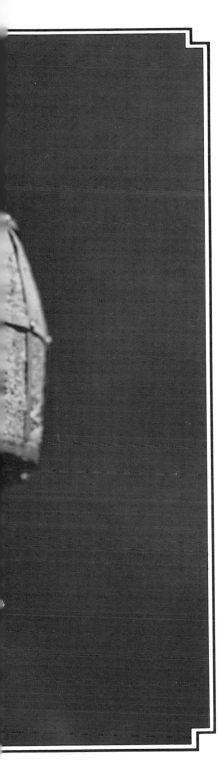

This Norse helmet dates from the migration period spanning the 6th to the 9th centuries A.D.

HISTORY

No immigrants were better prepared for the harsh demands of pioneer life than the Swedes. As early as the 9th century, a tradition of overseas exploration and territorial expansion was begun by Swedish and Norwegian sailors, called Vikings. Widely feared as brutal warriors, they also were courageous explorers who sailed unknown seas in their search for new worlds.

They were motivated in this quest by the brutal Scandinavian climate. Although Sweden boasts green meadows, birch trees, and wild flowers, it also endures frigid snowy winters and piercing winds. Fifteen percent of the country lies within the Arctic Circle, and some northern regions are covered by frost 12 months a year. Many of Sweden's early inhabitants did not survive infancy; those who did were toughened by the effort to wrest crops out of the unyielding soil. If they lasted into old age, when they could no longer contribute as much as they consumed, Swedes often sacrificed their lives by leaping off cliffs. Several places in Sweden still bear names that reflect this grim practice.

The continual struggle for sustenance explains why the Vikings conceived of heaven, which they called Valhalla, as a place where food was always plentiful. The Vikings' Swedish descendants, who departed for America in the 19th century, revived this dream. Valhalla offered a bottomless supply of mead (a fermented drink made of honey, yeast, malt, and water), and its resi-

17

Mythological beasts adorned many of the Vikings' high-prowed boats.

dents feasted on the boar Saehrimnir who, although roasted and eaten every night, appeared whole again the next morning.

Such Norse tales developed as part of an ancient oral tradition; that is, a storyteller or minstrel would amuse listeners with these sagas or sing them as part of an evening's entertainment. Gradually, some of this lore was written down, primarily by Snorri Sturluson, an Icelandic scholar and statesman of the early 13th century. Sturluson recognized how important these stories were to Scandinavia's cultural history and aimed to preserve as many of them as he could. Those left unwritten were lost but, due to Sturluson's work, many of the Vikings' sagas, which shed light on their ways and beliefs, still exist today.

Early History

Struggles for the throne dominated Sweden's history until the 13th century, when Jarl Birger, a scion of the influential Folkungar family, emerged as the country's most powerful ruler. A strong, intelligent leader, Birger founded Stockholm, still the nation's capital, and introduced reforms that soon enabled peasant farmers to shake off the bonds of serfdom. His successor, Magnus Ladulas, helped stabilize Sweden under a single king. Turmoil visited further generations of Swedish monarchs, as they—or their widows—staved off ambitious relatives.

Gradually, the bloodbaths ceased and, occasionally, enlightened leaders managed to help the country progress politically. In the 14th and 15th centuries, Sweden achieved some dramatic governmental reforms, including a national code that was formulated in 1350 to set forth the laws of the land. Any attacks in church, in the tribal courts, or against a defenseless woman, for example, branded the culprit as an outlaw, stripped of all rights and property.

This epoch saw great changes in foreign as well as domestic affairs. During the 14th century, Margaret, the daughter of Denmark's monarch, married the king of Norway, a neighboring country with territorial claims to Sweden. Upon the deaths of her husband and her father, Margaret assumed their titles. In 1389 she defeated Sweden's king in battle and established joint rule over Denmark, Sweden, and Norway. An able diplomat as well as monarch, she persuaded the legislatures of all three nations to accept her heir, Erik of Pomerania, as their king. Erik was crowned in the Swedish city of Kalmar in 1397. Thus, the famed Kalmar Union was formed.

His monarchy alarmed the Swedish people, however, and the angry Swedish nobles, who had lost much of their own political power to the king, incited the peasants to rebel. Only after Erik agreed to grant the nobles' requests did they allow him to reclaim the throne. When he failed to keep his promises, Denmark's governing council deposed him in 1438; the Swedish council followed suit a year later, and, in an attempt to ward off future transgressions, formed the Riksdag, a legislative body. Divided into four houses—nobles, clergy, burghers (townspeople), and yeomen—the Riksdag was empowered to make all subsequent political decisions.

Despite these reforms, Swedish unrest continued, culminating in the gruesome Bloodbath of Stockholm. This episode occurred in 1520 when Christian II, Denmark's king, seized control of Sweden by defeating in battle the Swedish regent (governor) Sten Sture the Younger. Following his victory, Christian assembled all the highest-ranking men of Sweden at his castle for a night of entertainment. But when the nobles, bishops, and burghers—the powers behind the Riksdag—were gathered in the great hall, its heavy doors clanged shut upon them and Christian had all 80 executed. Their corpses were piled up and burned outside the city walls.

Sweden's hopes for equitable rule were not entirely dashed, however. Gustav Vasa, kin to some of the Bloodbath's victims, soon learned of the slaughter and fled. Disguised as a peasant, he wandered from farm to

The sleek, narrow hulls of Viking ships sliced neatly through waves that often overwhelmed the vessels built by other seafaring peoples.

Kalmar Castle was the seat of Erik of Pomerania, who ruled the alliance that joined Sweden, Norway, and Denmark in 1397.

farm, a step ahead of Danish guards sent to kill him. By Christmas 1520 Gustav had reached the town of Rattvik where, in an old church, he publicly described Christian's act of betrayal and tried to rally the villagers to form a resistance army, offering to lead them himself. A total stranger to his auditors, Gustav failed to persuade them that his horrible account was true. He sadly strapped on his skis and set off for Norway and exile.

Shortly after his departure, news came from Stockholm confirming Gustav's tale. The Swedes now feared they had lost Gustav—and his leadership. Quickly, they dispatched their two fastest skiers to track him down. The race lasted 56 miles. Just before Gustav reached the Norwegian border, the skiers finally caught up to him. (This momentous event is still observed in Sweden with an annual ski race, the *Vasaloppet*, entered by hundreds of young Swedes.)

Gustav Vasa became one of Sweden's most powerful and important kings. He initiated wholesale changes, sorely needed by a nation beset with problems, including a depleted national treasury and an economy crippled by a century of political discord. Lacking any other options, Gustav turned to the Catholic church to refill Sweden's coffers. Year after year he borrowed money from the church in order to finance the government—until he had, in effect, plundered all of its extensive holdings.

This action incensed the nation's clergy, and Gustav realized that he could best justify himself by elevating the conflict to loftier grounds. He continued to appropriate ecclesiastical funds but joined the camp of the German reformer Martin Luther, whose followers decried the centralized power of the Roman Catholic church. Gustav complained that by using Latin, rather than Swedish, the Catholic masses slighted Swedish worshipers, who deserved to hear the divine Word preached in the language they themselves spoke. In 1527 he formally replaced the Catholic church with the Church of Sweden, headed by himself instead of the pope. Gustav seized virtually all church property, rechanneled its funds into the national treasury, and subordinated the clergy to the crown, a state of affairs that still exists in Sweden.

Although some Swedish Catholics objected to Gustav's tyranny over the church—eventually even Lutheran clergymen protested—the country prospered during his reign. He enabled the Swedish empire to grow and remained a popular ruler throughout his life. Indeed, he was so beloved that in 1544 the Riksdag voted to make Sweden's traditionally elective monarchy hereditary, so that the eldest child in each successive generation of Gustav's family would occupy the nation's throne. By the 1600s, under the leadership of Gustav's grandson, Gustav II Adolf, Sweden was recognized as a major military force in Europe. But when Gustav II died in battle in 1632, his sole heir was his six-year-old daughter, Christina, and nobles once again began to rule the country.

A Failed Colony

Seventeenth-century Sweden was a poor country, its finances drained by the government's aggressive foreign policy and overly ambitious military campaigns. One scheme set forth to rectify the problem was the initiation of a joint program of international trade and overseas colonization.

In 1637, backed with equal amounts of capital from Sweden and Holland, two Dutch merchants, Samuel

Before the advent of Lutheranism in the 16th century, the Catholic church played a dominant role in Swedish history.

Gustav Vasa (pictured here) rallied the Swedes to revolt against the tyrannical King Christian II in 1520.

Blommaert and Peter Minuit—who had purchased Manhattan Island from the Indians for $24 just 11 years earlier—founded the New Sweden Company. In 1638 the company sent two Swedish ships to settle the territory now called Wilmington, Delaware. The Swedes bought land there from the Indians, built a fort, naming it after their queen, Christina, and returned to Sweden with a cargo of tobacco and hides. But they failed to make a profit. Two years passed before a second expedition was launched, and this one faltered as badly as the first. By this time Sweden was involved, as was most of Europe, in the Thirty Years' War, and, its attention turned to greater matters, could muster little enthusiasm for its tiny, unprofitable trading outpost in the New World.

Galled by the apathy of their copartners, the Dutch investors wanted no further part of New Sweden and in 1641 sold their holdings to the Swedish government. For the next 10 years, Governor Johan Printz led the Christian community. It did well, although communication with the homeland was poor. Then, in 1655, Holland again entered the scene, reclaiming some of the colony's occupied land as its own. Backing this appropriation with force, they captured the settlement. The loss to Sweden was minor; the colony had never become truly profitable. The successor to Queen Christina—her cousin, Karl Gustav—made no further attempt to colonize the Americas. Nor did his successors.

The Modern Era

The 18th century in Europe is often referred to as the Age of Enlightenment because people began to pay more attention to the ideas of independent thinkers than to the doctrine propagated by the Christian churches. Views of the natural world were reshaped by the scientific discoveries of Isaac Newton (1642–1727) and James Watt (1736–1819). At the same time, individual freedom gained new meaning from the philosophical arguments of the Frenchmen Voltaire (1694–1778) and Jean-Jacques Rousseau (1712–78) and the Englishman John Locke (1632–1704). Their ideas bred a new vision of politics and civilization that ultimately guided revolutionary passions in Europe and in the American colonies.

In Sweden this new age gave birth to an increased fascination with science and technology. Sweden has always been among the leaders of technological production, and as early as 1730 it enjoyed a golden age of scientific research. During this era, 10 new chemical elements were first identified in Sweden, and Swedish scientists made further contributions in the fields of physics, mineralogy, astronomy, biology, and medicine.

Gustav Vasa's grandson, Gustav II made Sweden a military power.

These investigations often took them to remote places. Just as the Vikings had crossed oceans a thousand years before, 18th-century Swedes traveled to North and South America and to the Pacific, where they conducted geographical explorations. Swedish army officers who ventured as far as Siberia and the Far East made invaluable maps charting these new territories.

Not all Swedes basked in the glories of the age, however. Farmers, for instance, faced a shortage of land, and poor harvests added to their woes. Drastic inflation weakened the economy, and it was not uncommon to see bands of beggars roaming the Swedish countryside. These hardships, continuing into the 19th century, eventually spurred a massive wave of emigration.

Other factors, too, demoralized the Swedes. One was widespread disenchantment of the country's popu-

In the mid-17th century, the Thirty Years' War exacted a heavy toll on Sweden's population and finances. This woodcut depicts the Battle of Nördlingen, which the Swedes lost in 1634.

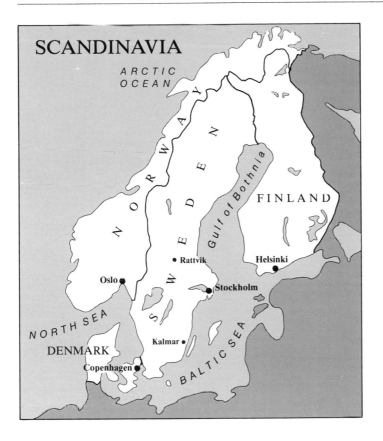

SCANDINAVIA

ARCTIC OCEAN

NORTH SEA

NORWAY

SWEDEN

Gulf of Bothnia

FINLAND

• Rattvik

Helsinki •

Oslo •

Stockholm •

DENMARK

Kalmar •

BALTIC SEA

Copenhagen •

lace with their government. Hard-line Lutherans had advocated the persecution of dissenters such as the members of a new spiritual sect, the Pietists. The Pietists believed that religious experience should emphasize worshipers' personal involvement in Christianity rather than the authority of the church. To counter the Pietists, the official ministry sponsored the 1726 Conventicle Act, outlawing all religious meetings except those sanctioned by the state church. The act was repealed in 1858, but its repressive effects lingered for generations.

Another issue was more directly political. The Swedish people had wearied of partisan feuds that seemed an outgrowth of parliamentary rule. Even as American colonists girded themselves to rebel against the British king, a revolution to strengthen the Swedish crown brewed in Stockholm. In 1772 Gustav III led an

In 1638, the New Sweden Company sent two ships to the New World, starting a colony near Wilmington, Delaware.

army that revolted against the parliament, thus restoring power to the monarchy without spilling any blood.

Only 26 years old, Gustav envisioned greatness for his country and brimmed with enthusiasm for bettering the conditions of his subjects. During his first 15 years on the throne, he lowered tariffs, improved the country's monetary system and public finances, modernized its military defense, and gave worshipers more freedom of expression. It was at this time that the idealistic yet practical Gustav recognized the newly formed United States of America and negotiated the treaty of 1782.

These triumphs, however, did not lessen the devastation wrought by a series of famines. Coupled with mounting uneasiness about the king's increasing power, the famines bred discontent among powerful nobles. These nobles, initially Gustav's allies, became disillusioned with him in 1789, when the monarch introduced a new constitution that strengthened royal authority and eroded the nobility's privileges. In 1792, at a masked ball held in Stockholm's opera house, an assassin ended Gustav's controversial reign.

The country Gustav had ruled for two decades was a study in contrasts: Cultural progress coexisted with misery among the working classes; opportunities available to the middle class and farmers were offset by the grumblings of the nobility—Gustav semed to have created a nation of contradictions. Not that all Sweden's difficulties were the monarch's fault; no kingly wisdom could ease the shortage of arable land. This scarcity was the major problem faced by the many farmers who made up the first wave of immigrants to America.

Queen Christina (seated at right), supported Sweden's only attempt at colonizing North America.

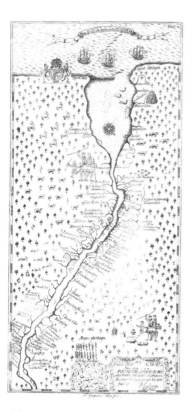

This 1702 engraving charts Sweden's holdings in present-day Pennsylvania.

In 1796 Gustav's son, Gustav IV Adolf (1778–1837), assumed the throne, on the eve of wars that would engulf Europe for a generation. Because Sweden valued its trading ties to England, the young king sided with the British and Russians against the French, led by Napoléon Bonaparte. The early campaigns favored the latter, and a temporary alliance between France and Russia in 1807 resulted in Russia's invasion of Finland. In 1809 Sweden was forced to yield all its Finnish holdings—including some that had been Swedish possessions as far back as prehistoric times—along with the northeasternmost strip of Sweden. In all, the country lost more than one-third of its territory, land it had owned for more than six centuries. Angered and humiliated, the Swedish people made King Gustav IV their scapegoat, deposing him in a bloodless revolution. He finished his life as a lonely outcast, penniless and anonymous.

After unseating the king, Sweden adopted a new constitution influenced by one that had recently been drawn up by America's founders. It restored the balance between the monarch and parliament, guaranteed freedom of the press, and granted all citizens access to public records. It also provided for the investigation of any public servant accused of corruption or mismanagement. The king was still the head executive, and the Riksdag continued to consist of the four estates: nobles, clergy, burghers, and farmers. This constitution, adopted in 1809, remained in effect until 1974.

The Napoleonic Wars concluded in 1815, followed by an economic slump. In Sweden, these troubles coincided with a resurgence of political and fiscal reform. By midcentury the system of medieval guilds gave way to free enterprise, ending the trade monopoly that towns had held for centuries. In 1847 the government lifted a long-standing ban against exports and imports; other reforms included rights for single women, a more humane penal code, local self-government, and more

religious liberty. Further concessions were granted more slowly, and the two main issues that dominated politics in the late 19th century went unaddressed: the demand that the land tax be terminated, and the demand that obligatory military duty be abolished as well. It was not until 1892 that these issues were resolved – and by then thousands of Swedes had chosen a new life in the new land across the seas. ➤

The Riksdag, a legislative body formed in 1438, includes representatives from Sweden's various political parties.

In 1905, a family in Dalarne,
Sweden, packs up all its
belongings for the trip to America.

THE OPPORTUNITY OF LAND

In the 19th century many Swedes had grown dissatisfied with life in their homeland. Some sought better opportunities by moving to larger cities within the country's borders, but most realized that grander possibilities awaited them across the ocean. Even at the beginning of the immigration wave, when Swedes only dimly grasped the reality of conditions in North America, vaunting newspaper stories and the glowing reports of Swedish-American Episcopal minister Gustav Unonius (1810–1902) enticed many Swedes to emigrate.

Much as the romance of an exotic and distant country attracted Swedes, they also had practical reasons for trying their luck there. The United States offered available land, wide-scale employment, religious tolerance, and freedom from mandatory military service. Many years later, a Swedish American explained his reasons for immigration in terms that probably echoed the views held by others. "I cannot give the exact reason for emigrating," this Pennsylvania coal miner wrote in 1905. "The problem of bread was probably the main one; class differences and the question of personal worth. I felt as if I were useless, both to the community and myself. My word was nothing, even when it concerned my own soul."

A farmer harvests oats near Lerdal, Sweden, in 1905. The shortage of arable land forced many farmers off their family plots.

The scarcity of arable land in Sweden became a crisis in the 19th century, when the nation's mortality rate had shrunk, thanks to improved medical care, healthier living conditions, and longer periods without warfare. This increased the population at a rate greater than in previous centuries—it more than doubled, from 2.3 million people in 1800 to about 5.5 million in 1910.

As the population grew, there was less space to accommodate it. Farmers had an especially difficult time. Many lived on family-operated plots that passed down generationally. The system worked except when there were too many offspring, each awaiting his own share of the farm. The solution was either to bequeath the entire spread to the eldest son—forcing his brothers to hire themselves out as laborers—or to parcel out a morsel of land to each. An added difficulty was that long years of farming had depleted the soil of minerals, reducing its productivity.

A further problem was Sweden's natural terrain. A rocky country, its fields often needed to be cleared, and some sections were chronically resistant to crop growing. A pattern of bad weather multiplied these hardships: In the 1840s Sweden alternately suffered droughts and torrential showers. Some harvests grew moldy from an excess of rain; others produced inadequate yields because the land was parched. The combined result was devastating famine, worsened by the population explosion. Starving, oppressed, and land-poor, farmers began to look for sustenance elsewhere. America—a huge country with, it was said, enough land for everyone—beckoned to many. As early as 1817, Sweden's foremost poet, Esaias Tegner, had written: "Is it true what so many say that the day darkens for old Europe? Far to the West beyond the sea, where the sun sets for us, there does it rise for a happier world. There Europe has already sent many of her best hopes."

When the United States government opened the midwestern and western plains states for settlement, enormous opportunities awaited the Swedes. Here was a vast country avid for settlers to clear and farm the land. For most of the 19th century, America welcomed people from all over Europe. They provided the labor necessary to expand and then settle the U.S. frontier. In the forefront were immigrants from Sweden, a country that ranked eighth among European nations in the total number of natives who left its borders.

The United States and Canada offered more than farming opportunities to hopeful immigrants. Over-population in Sweden had created an enormous class of landless farm workers in search of employment. Most European countries readily adapted to the Industrial Revolution of the mid-18th century, but Sweden reacted tardily. In 1848 only 8 percent of its labor force had industrial jobs, compared with the 80 percent who supported themselves by farming. As the century progressed, Sweden was held back further by its dearth of coal, a substance crucial for steam-powered industries.

The rising population of the unemployed turned to America, whose railroad companies and construction firms sent agents to Sweden in order to contract for jobs

Johan Printz governed New Sweden in the 1640s.

with immigrant workers. Many Swedes gratefully accepted the offer to work for Americans who wanted—and needed—their services.

Freedom and Equality

Economic opportunity was only one cause of Swedish immigration. Another was the desire to practice freedom of religious choice. Swedes, who were mostly Lutheran by birth, could leave the state church only through formal petition. Even after the repeal of the Conventicle Act in 1858, many Swedes still complained that the church, because it was subordinate to the state, had grown increasingly secular in its concerns. At the same time, Christianity in America was undergoing a revivalist movement that created a truly committed community of religious believers.

At least two religious groups left Sweden in large numbers: the Janssonists, a revivalist Lutheran sect; and the Mormons, mostly former Lutherans converted by the proselytizing efforts of American missionaries. (The long-lasting success of Mormon proselytizing was confirmed by the 1980 U.S. census, which showed that 5.8 percent of the population of Utah—the seat of Mormonism—claimed Swedish ancestors. Utah, moreover, contains the third-highest concentration—after Minnesota and Nebraska—of Swedish Americans.)

In addition to religious complaints, Swedes voiced displeasure with their country's social inequality. Class divisions had been cemented with the foundation of the Riksdag, which placed power securely in the hands of nobles, clergy, merchants, and landowners—who sometimes had more than one vote each. The poor, the landless, and laborers, on the other hand, had no electoral say. The United States had class distinctions, too, but they were less rigid and not enforced by law. As one immigrant from Småland wrote in 1868: "Here we have rich men, here we have learned men, here we have smart men, here we have bosses who sometimes work us like dogs—but *masters* we have none."

Still other Swedes may have emigrated in order to escape military conscription. All Swedish males were required to serve a term in the armed services. Though not long at first, these terms increased steadily throughout the century. In 1857 military service meant 30 days' duty; it grew to 45 days in 1885. Many 19th-century Swedish youths viewed conscription as an invasion of their personal rights. Worse yet, duty in the armed services routinely meant mistreatment at the hands of upper-class officers bent on reinforcing Sweden's class divisions.

Colonial Immigrants

Even before the mass migration of the 19th century, Sweden had made its mark on North America by founding New Sweden, a colony near Wilmington, Delaware that was the first permanent settlement in the Delaware River valley. From the beginning, the Swedes displayed the enthusiasm that later helped them tame the Midwest and the Pacific Northwest. "A remarkably

In the 18th century, Swedish Americans built the first churches in the Delaware River valley. This one is situated in Wilmington.

beautiful country," wrote the colony's governor, Johan Printz, in 1643. "It has all the glories that any human being on earth can ever desire. . . . Such a splendid country as this, endowed with all kinds of wonderful things, I have never seen. Nothing is wanting, except means, diligence and seriousness in the continuation of this work."

Swedes built the first churches in the Delaware Valley and introduced the log cabin to North America, using techniques they brought across the Atlantic from the northern timberlands of their country. More importantly, at least for future Swedish immigrants, these pioneers established cultural and religious links between the two countries. "The Indians and we are as one people; we live in much greater friendship with them than with the English," reported the Reverend Eric Bjorck, a Swedish Lutheran minister, in 1697.

The mutual admiration between America and Sweden was intensified by two women. Fredrika Bremer (1801–65) was a novelist whose depictions of Swedish family life were widely read in the United States. When

When Sweden lengthened the term of enforced military service, many young men left for America.

she crossed the Atlantic for a tour, she was invited by the American poet James Russell Lowell to stay with him and his family in Cambridge, Massachusetts; following her three-week visit, he confessed, "I do not *like* her, I *love* her." She similarly enchanted American writers Nathaniel Hawthorne and Washington Irving. Bremer also created quite a stir in the homeland when she remarked in 1853, "What a glorious new Scandinavia might not Minnesota become! Here would the Swede find again his clear, romantic lakes, the plains of Scania rich in corn, and the vallies of Norrland . . . their hunting field and their fisheries . . ."

Jenny Lind (1820–87), "the Swedish nightingale," caused an even greater sensation when she arrived for a concert tour in 1850. Her performances were sellouts that sometimes ended in riots. Later, she organized funds and emptied her own pockets to help ease the transition of Swedish immigrants arriving in America.

By the middle of the 19th century, the time was ripe for the Swedish people to try their luck in this country that had so warmly welcomed their countrywomen. The ongoing admiration between Swedes and Americans made it possible for Swedish immigrants to arrive in the New World with some sense of an existing connection.

Even so, many newcomers arrived with misconceptions about America. This problem was addressed in Vilhelm Moberg's popular novel, *The Emigrants* (1948). Its deluded characters glean their knowledge of the promised land solely from an erroneous book about North America and from spurious legends circulated in Sweden. The emigrants are told, for instance, that American farmland contains no stones and that they need never obey any authority other than themselves. Sadly, these falsehoods gained the authority of truth and clouded the views of immigrants who sometimes overlooked the genuine opportunities open to them in the New World and complained instead of disappointment.

Jenny Lind, "the Swedish Nightingale," drew sellout crowds during her 1850 American concert tour.

Many Swedes made the 10-week voyage to America on cargo ships that charged $12–$15 per passenger.

Toward the Unknown

When the first rush of immigrants started in the 1840s and 1850s, mothers began packing their family's chests with clothes and tools and household goods. As they folded their weaving and chose which spindles and bobbins to take, they contemplated the new life ahead of them. Moberg's novel vividly describes these preparations:

> Now [the chest] is pulled out into the daylight once more; it was the roomiest and strongest packing case they could find—five feet long, three feet high, wrought with strong iron bands three fingers wide. . . . The four oak walls of this chest were for thousands of miles to enclose and protect their essentials; to these planks would be entrusted most of their belongings. . . . And the ancient clothes chest which was about to pass into

an altogether new and eventful epoch of its history was even given a new name in its old age. It was called the 'America chest'. . .

The middle of the 19th century brought thousands of Swedes to American shores. Many took advantage of the relatively cheap fares—$12–$15 per person—available on cargo ships laden with iron ore. Because these ships furnished no meals, the passengers had to supply their own food, enough to last for the 7- to 10-week voyage. This added expense was so high that it limited passenger lists to landed farmers, skilled artisans, and industrial workers.

After docking in New York City, most Swedes continued westward to settlements in Wisconsin and Illinois. Many traveled by rail or boat along the Erie Canal to Buffalo, then by boat across the Great Lakes to the prairieland of the Upper Mississippi Valley or to Chicago. The entire journey took four or five months and often exhausted a family's entire savings, as Hans Mattson remembered when thinking back to the arrival of his fellow Swedes in Illinois. Mattson recalled seeing

the poor immigrant . . . just landed from a steamer, in his short jacket and other outlandish costume, perhaps seated on a wooden box, with his wife and a large group of children around him, wondering how he shall

Castle Garden, in New York Harbor, was the port of entry for most European immigrants, including those from Sweden.

be able to raise enough means to get himself ten or twenty miles into the country, or to redeem the bedding and other household goods which he has perchance left in Milwaukee as a pledge for his railroad and steamboat ticket. . . . Poor, bewildered, ignorant and odd looking, he had been an object of pity and derision all the way from Gothernberg or Christiania to the little cabin of a country-man of his, where he found rest and shelter until he could build one of his own.

Upon arriving at their new homes, all the adults in the family usually tried to find work: the men as farm laborers, on the railroads, or in construction; the women as maids if unmarried, or, if married, by taking in washing. Within two or three years they hoped to meet their family goal—amassing enough savings to purchase a farm.

Swedes introduced the log cabin to America and built the sturdy structures throughout the Midwest.

Letters Back Home

Once Swedes had settled in America, they mailed reports to their friends and families in Sweden; such correspondence and also newspaper accounts made a keen impression on a country plagued with overpopulation, unemployment, and, eventually, famine. Letters from the New World often used rosier terms than actual conditions warranted. Accuracy, it seemed, mattered less than other considerations. Some immigrants were too proud to admit failure; some feared those at home would be alarmed by tales of hardship. As a result, the settlers who followed the first waves of adventurers received a rude awakening when they stepped off the boat. "We often find that he who . . . describes the beautiful carriage he owns," wrote one disappointed

This engraving shows the Erie Canal's system of locks in Lockport, New York. Many pioneers boated on the Erie Canal until they reached the Great Lakes.

In the mid-19th century, Hans Mattson wrote movingly of the hardships faced by Swedish pioneers. Here he poses in the native costume of India.

immigrant, "is the owner of a wheelbarrow for which he himself serves as the locomotive." Another deluded immigrant, who arrived in 1843 on the strength of enthusiastic letters from earlier settlers, found that "their home was much poorer than any charcoal hut in Sweden, without floor, almost without roof, and with a few stones in a corner which were supposed to be a stove. Such was the magnificent house which they had written they were building to receive all the Swedes who would come, . . ." But these letters of complaint, as frank as they were, failed to stem the tide of Swedish immigrants washing upon America's shores.

One early settler sent back accounts that were unusually influential in the homeland. Gustav Unonius was not the first Swedish American to mail home enthusiastic letters, but his accounts of life in the United States led many Swedes to chance a new start in the promised land. Unonius arrived in the United States in 1841 at the age of 31, accompanied by his wife, Charlotte. They landed in New York City. Then, with some friends and their maidservant, they traveled by boat up the Hudson River, along the Erie Canal, and across the Great Lakes—no railroads as yet reached the Midwest. Thirty miles west of Milwaukee, Wisconsin, they founded New Uppsala, a community on the shores of Pine Lake. The beauty of the area filled Unonius with enthusiasm, and he gave expression to it in glowing letters published in *Aftonbladet*, a Swedish newspaper read by thousands of Swedes and even some Danes and Norwegians. Some of his readers were idle dreamers and deluded romantics ill equipped for frontier hardships. But even the more practical and hardy of those who came often succumbed to the bitter midwestern winters and to fatal diseases. Cholera and malaria, in particular, claimed the lives of many children.

At last Unonius's own pioneering spirit flagged, and after a few years in New Uppsala, he left and entered a nearby Episcopal seminary. In 1845 he was ordained and began his new career as minister to Scandinavian settlements in Wisconsin. Often his family was left alone while he visited his distant parishioners. Later, he held a five-year ministry in Chicago, where he helped organize a Swedish-Norwegian Episcopal congregation and worked to aid the rising tide of Scandinavian immigrants. Exhausted by the sacrifices demanded by their new homeland—Unonius and his wife buried five of their children—the couple returned to Sweden in 1858, after 17 years. The minister soon plunged into his memoirs, which were published in America in two volumes (1861–62). A major document about the Midwest, Unonius's book finally appeared in an English translation 100 years after its original publication.

Unonius's memoirs range over many topics. He criticizes religious sects that differ from his own and rebukes some Americans for taking advantage of the bewildered masses who came to their country in good faith. His affection for the New World surfaces when he describes the Wisconsin and Illinois prairies and in his praise of America's democratic principles. Unonius writes shrewdly about the problems of immigration, cautioning his compatriots against hasty and uninformed decisions. America is indeed a land of opportunity, he concludes, but one that demands laborious efforts from those who wish to prosper there.

Group Settlements

Men such as Unonius provided leadership to immigrant settlements—groups of immigrant whole families that traveled as a ready-made community. These units were largely responsible for opening America's heartlands, beginning with western Illinois. They were not the first settlers in that state, large areas of which had already attracted Americans from New England and from the South. But many Swedes came to Illinois in its formative years, including those who followed Eric Jansson to Bishop Hill, a religious community founded in 1846.

Jansson had first left Sweden because the illegal revivalist sect he originated branded him as an outlaw in

After immigrating in 1841, Gustav Unonius sent back many letters describing his experiences. Published in the Swedish press, they persuaded thousands to risk a new start in North America.

An elderly woman contributes to the commune of Bishop Hill by making use of skills brought over from Sweden.

the service of the devil. After a brief exile in Norway, Jansson came to America in 1846 with his wife, two children, and some of his followers. In his Illinois settlement, Bishop Hill, all worked together to build and farm and to create, they hoped, a perfect society. The inhabitants of Bishop Hill shared everything—from meals and worship to property and workloads. The first winter was harsh, but by the spring of 1847, the settlers gazed upon fields of flax, corn, and wheat. The commune's religious fervor slackened following Jansson's murder in 1850, but Bishop Hill became known as a model farm and as an agricultural center. An economic crisis in 1857 persuaded the commune's leaders to end the experiment, but many of its charter members moved on to create successful farms elsewhere. Bishop Hill—the second-oldest Swedish settlement and the only completely Swedish-built community in America—can be visited today as a living example of 19th-century Swedish-American pioneer life.

Other Areas of Swedish Concentration

Another famous destination for Swedish immigrants came to be called Swede Town, an area in northwest Chicago, the city that had attracted Swedes almost since it came into existence in 1837. Chicago Swedes built their own wooden houses and churches and contributed their carpentry skills to the construction of many local buildings. In the early 1850s, however, a cholera epidemic dramatically reduced the number of Swedish residents. According to one estimate, two-thirds of its 1854 immigrants died of this dread disease.

Chicago was important not only as settlement but also as the way station for many Swedes who then went on to other midwestern and western areas. Minnesota, for instance, had attracted Swedes as early as 1810, when woodsman and trapper Jacob Falstrom staked his homestead there. In 1851 an immigrant community was founded near Chisago Lake, leading to a major concentration of Swedes in Chisago County. This area, along with the neighboring county of Isanti, became the most Swedish of all districts in America. By 1860 a U.S. census reported that the number of Swedes in Minnesota had grown to almost 3,200, a total surpassed only by the 17,500 Germans and 8,400 Norwegians. By the early 1900s the Swedes were the biggest foreign-born group in Minnesota.

Mid-19th-century Swedish settlements stretched all across Michigan, Indiana, and Ohio. Michigan's Upper Peninsula offered farmland, of course, and also employment in mines, as well as in the lumber and railroad industries. Initially, Indiana welcomed an even greater number of Swedish settlers, but eventually many of them moved on to the bordering states of Michigan and Illinois.

The immigrants did not stop in the Midwest but pushed even farther onward, reaching as far as the California coast. Indeed, it was a Swede, Gustavus M. Waseurtz of Sandels, who actually discovered the gold deposit that led to the legendary gold rush of 1848. In 1844 Waseurtz found the precious ore on land owned by Johann August Sutter, who ignored the news, pointing out that his own harvest and other matters kept him too busy to prospect for buried riches. Four years passed before the California gold rush began, and it was Sutter, not Waseurtz, whose name went down in history.

Other western areas also attracted immigrants from Sweden. In 1838, S. N. Swenson built a ranch in Texas and within 10 years had lured some of his countrymen to work on it as contract laborers. And several hundred Swedish immigrants who had been converted to Mormonism by American missionaries traveled to Utah, where the church had its headquarters.

The American Civil War

In 1861 Swedish Americans fought in the Civil War. Some joined the Confederate army, but most sided with the Union. One young Swede, a volunteer writing to his minister father, expressed the feelings of many when he wrote, "I have come to the conclusion lately to try to do something for my country and for the poor African race. . . . I think this cause is just and a righteous war and should I meet my death on the battlefield I feel I shall die in a glorious cause."

Swedes had never been owned outright as slaves, but many had suffered under oppressive masters in their homeland and sympathized mightily with American blacks. By the late 1850s, Swedish Americans had become vitally interested in the slavery issue. In the Midwest, they intently followed the debates between

Stephen A. Douglas and Abraham Lincoln, and Swedish-American support for Lincoln's 1860 presidential campaign reached a fever pitch. Those Swedes who had settled in the South generally backed the seceding Confederate states, but no more than 50 Swedish-born men served in the rebel army. On either side, the Swedes

Farming was a family occupation in America, just as it had been in the old country.

made good officers and soldiers; some had received military training before immigrating, but even those without such experience were often strapping young farmers who adapted easily to the rigorous discipline of army life.

When the war began, about 20,000 Swedish Americans lived in the North; of these, approximately 3,000 enlisted for military service, the greatest numbers hailing from Illinois and Minnesota. At least 75 Swedish-born officers served in the Union army, often leading troops primarily composed of fellow Swedes. Scandinavian units were formed in the East and Midwest. The most impressive unit was the Fifteenth Wisconsin Regiment: Of its 900 men, most were from Norway, but there were also many Swedes and some Danes. By the war's end, six Swedish-born Civil War veterans were awarded the U.S. Congressional Medal of Honor, the country's highest military decoration. One Swedish American, a member of the Eighty-second Illinois Regiment, received a special citation from President

(continued on page 57)

Some newcomers sought work in mines such as this huge open pit in Hibbing, Minnesota.

THE PUSH WEST

Kraus.
at 70. 1908.

The primitivist canvases of Olof Krans, painted around 1900, depict pioneers clearing land, sowing crops, and whisking through the countryside in an ox-drawn sled. In J. S. Curry's Wisconsin Landscape, rain clouds cast shadows over the bright patchwork of a thriving farm.

In the 1870s and 1880s, railroad companies issued brochures and pamphlets that enticed settlers to western territories. North Dakota, portrayed in two advertisements as an alluring goddess, offered free land to hardy Swedish Americans willing to build farms from scratch.

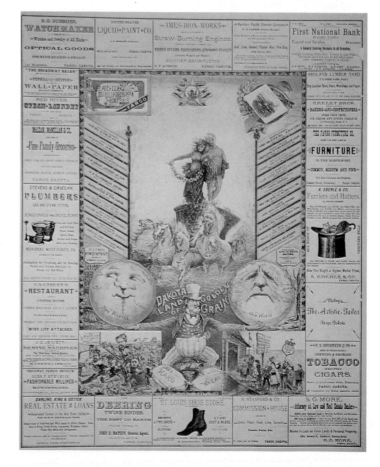

John Gast's 1873 painting American Progress *celebrates the nation's transcontinental push, as pioneers and prospectors trek west by boat, covered wagon, stagecoach, and railroad.*

Today, Bishop Hill, an Illinois settlement founded in 1846 by religious dissident Eric Jannsson, is an authentic reminder of Swedish-American pioneer life.

(continued from page 48)

Lincoln. This was Mans Olsson Lindbergh, whose grandson, Charles Lindbergh, later made aviation history.

Of all Swedish-born participants in the American Civil War, none made a greater contribution than that of ship designer John Ericsson. His career began in his native country, where he designed mechanically operated ships intended to defend that country's vulnerable coastline. After coming to the United States, he drew up plans for the *Princeton*, a 600-ton Navy frigate made of iron, rather than the customary wood, and the first propeller-driven man-of-war ever constructed. His most famous ship, however, was the *Monitor*, designed in 1862. A small, low-floating vessel described by contemporaries as a "hat set on a shingle" or a "cheesebox

After the 1860s, many pioneers traveled across the continent by rail.

In 1862, John Ericsson designed the Monitor, *an ironclad ship that changed the course of naval strategy.*

on a raft," the *Monitor* outmaneuvered the Southern ironclad ship, the *Merrimack*, in the Civil War's most memorable naval contest. Thousands of spectators journeyed to the Virginia shore to watch the four-hour duel, which ended in a draw and signaled a new phase in naval combat.

Once peace resumed, full-scale immigration from Sweden started up anew, sparked by three successive crop failures there (1867–69) and by a rapid growth in the country's population, which soared from 4 million to 5.8 million and sent—during the 50 years following the Civil War—more than 1 million Swedes to America. In the 5 years from 1868 to 1873, 125,000 Swedes came to the United States. Some were mechanics, blacksmiths, carpenters, tailors, machinists, and shoemakers, but most were farmers lured by the Homestead Act of 1862.

This landmark legislation stated that men and women willing to break and work the land could own their own spread of 160 acres. The idea of free land boggled the minds of the Swedes, inhabitants of a country where family holdings had grown smaller and smaller and where poor weather conditions had caused years of agricultural disaster and relentless famine. Suddenly they could travel to a country with hundreds of acres waiting to be farmed. Once again boatloads of Swedes set out for the promised land. Most came prepared for the hardships involved in clearing new territory. Their expectations found a voice in the Reverend Olaf Olsson, who arrived in America in 1869 and shortly thereafter wrote home:

> We do not dig gold with pocket knives, we do not expect to become bountifully rich in a few days or in a few years, but what we aim at is to own our own homes, where each one has his own property, which with God's blessings will provide him with the sustenance which he and his family need. We are like the old Swedish yeoman in our freedom and independence.

. . . The advantage which America offers is not to make everyone rich at once, without toil and trouble, but the advantage is that the poor, who will and are able to work, secure a large piece of good land almost without cost, that they can work up little by little.

Realistic expectations were not all that prepared Swedes for the task of settling the unclaimed areas of the United States and Canada. The extensive logging experience many had already gained in the dense woodlands of their homeland uniquely qualified them to handle the strenuous chore of felling trees and building sturdy houses. Unlike so many other immigrants, Swedish homesteaders did not have to learn new trades; they simply honed skills they already possessed. Thus they made ideal pioneers. As one immigrant in Minnesota noted in a letter home to a relative, "The Swedes are highly valued as workers, so highly even that if you go and ask for work they may ask if you are Swedish, in that case you get work right away."

Gold discovered near Sutter's Mill, in the Sacramento Valley, triggered the California gold rush of 1848.

Urban Emigration

In the mid-1870s Swedish emigration rates dipped once again because of an upsurge in Sweden's economy marked by intensified railroad construction, higher production of lumber, iron, textiles, and machinery, and growing foreign trade. As long as business was booming, few Swedes felt impelled to seek a new life abroad.

By the decade's end, however, the emigration rate swelled again and stayed high until the early 1890s. This second great wave was unique because it included a high percentage of emigrants from urban areas. Many

The 1862 Homestead Act attracted settlers with the promise of free acreage in South Dakota and other western territories.

came from Stockholm, where a population increase of almost 50 percent—much of it caused by new arrivals from farms—had placed great strains on Sweden's capital city, causing unemployment, declining wages, and labor shortages. For the first time, Swedish immigrants flocked not only to America's rural heartlands but also to New England and New York City, industrial centers that needed urban workers trained in technical crafts such as ironwork.

At the same time, good tracts of land became a scarce commodity. By the last decade of the 19th century, only one frontier remained for the Swedish pioneers: Canada. When the Canadian Pacific Railroad had been completed, it opened up for settlement the vast territories of Manitoba, Saskatchewan, Alberta, and British Columbia. Lured by offers similar to the

Swedish industrial workers, hard-pressed to find employment in their homeland, flocked to American cities, such as Seattle, Washington, where jobs were plentiful.

Gold lured Swedish prospectors to the Alaska Yukon in the 1890s.

United States Homestead Act of 1862, many Swedes moved across the borders of Minnesota and North Dakota into the Canadian provinces. The Klondike gold rush from 1896 to 1900 pulled even more Swedes northward into the Yukon Territory and Alaska.

Just as they had done earlier in the United States, Swedes served as Canada's pioneers in the western territories. They chopped down trees, cleared land, built houses, and formed communities. Within 25 years the 25,000 Swedes in Canada had almost completely finished their pioneering work. The final frontier had been settled. As one dejected Swedish Canadian lamented in 1910:

> The best time for emigration is now past; all the valuable land is now taken. If there should possibly be a few thousands farms left, these are only a drop in the bucket, the ever-broadening stream of emigration

devours everything in its path. America had for long periods and up to the present been a fortunate place for emigrants. To get a considerable and fertile piece of land at little cost is certainly a great gain. With this land, many have brought themselves up to independent circumstances here; many have attained prosperity. In Canada an overwhelming flood of land-seekers is expected next year—several hundred thousand, the newspapers say. Canada is where they are coming, for in the States all the land is taken up. But already last year large crowds of disappointed persons had to pass this place by. The province is already inhabited up to one hundred miles north of the northernmost railroad in Canada. The climate is too cold and all agriculture north of the fifty-second parallel must be unprofitable. So it appears at present.

Once land became scarce in the United States, pioneers trekked north into the Canadian wilderness.

The Last Wave

In the 20th century, the last major influx of immigrants arrived; it lasted until 1929 when the stock market crash and then the Great Depression made economic opportunities no more plentiful in America than in Sweden.

Early in the century, Sweden had undergone dramatic changes. In 1905 Norway announced that the Swedish-Norwegian alliance was dissolved, a proclamation that nearly led to war. And in 1909, Sweden's massive labor problems culminated in a general strike involving 300,000 workers. Although the unions lost the battle, the voice of labor gained enough strength to force concessions from the government.

Still the New World beckoned, and Swedes left for America in search of better economic opportunities. This newest exodus caused a crisis in Sweden, which needed a full labor force because it was stepping up international trade and undergoing wide-scale industrialization. In 1904 two bills meant to restrict emigra-

By the early 1900s, Chicago had a booming Swede Town.

tion were introduced into the Swedish parliament. Three years later a commission of inquiry was charged with determining why so many Swedes had left the country.

The commission issued a questionnaire to Swedish Americans. One typical response served to describe their shared experience:

> I left my parents' home the 4th of April, 1871, and landed in New York the 4th of May the same year. Now, at last I was in the land of promises, without relatives, without friends, and almost without money. I wandered about like a deaf and dumb man. My ticket was to Chicago and I started for that city. . . . As in a dream I went up and down the streets in Chicago. Was this the so highly praised America?
>
> At last I left Chicago and went to Pennsylvania, where I worked on the railroads for about four years. Than I married a girl from my own home country. She had a little money and I had saved some, so we bought a small place of 10 acres, which we started to work up, bought three cows, one horse, and some farm implements. We kept this place for two years, when we sold it and bought another of 120 acres for $1,000. I sold 50 acres of this and that made us free from debt. Now we worked on this farm for a couple of years, when a sawmill in our neighborhood was offered for sale and we bought it for $2,000. Now I sawed timber both for myself and others, so within two years I had paid for the mill, but then it burned down and I had no insurance. I built up the mill immediately and started to saw again. Now I started to buy larger and smaller pieces of woodland and all went well. I sold my old place, bought a bigger and better one, started a country store, bought building lots in the cities, and started to build houses in Youngsville and Jamestown, New York. Today I have 300 acres of land, a good farm, a good sawmill with planing machinery; two stores, eight city houses, and ten lessees, who pay me $900 a year. . . . If I had remained in Sweden I should probably be a hired man, or at most a dependent farmer.

This man's progress—from initial disorientation and poverty to great prosperity—duplicated the experiences of many of his compatriots. It awakened the Swedish Commission of Inquiry to the realization that most emigrants had left Sweden looking for opportunities they simply couldn't find at home.

From 1914 to 1918, World War I virtually halted any travel on the high seas, and emigration did not resume until after the war, reaching its highest postwar figures in 1923. The great movement soon ended, however, as Sweden, like many European countries, took significant strides toward accommodating its citizens and treating them more equitably. In 1919 the 48-hour workweek went into effect in Sweden, and by 1921 all men and women could vote in general elections. It was a time of new possibilities, and there was less need to cross the ocean to start their lives anew. Then, in 1929, the stock market crashed and the economy of the western world tumbled, taking everyone with it. The "Golden Door" had closed.

By 1929 a total of almost 1.3 million Swedes had weathered the voyage across the Atlantic to America. Traces of those immigrants still appear—in the names of towns and cities, in familiar surnames such as Swanson, Anderson, and Johnson, in the beautiful craft work sustained over generations.

The Progressive Politics of Swedish Farmers

When Swedish immigrants and their descendants settled in America's heartland in the 19th century, they brought ideas of democratic social reform that had an important impact on future American politics. By the early 1870s, the newly formed Riksdag of their homeland was already enacting remarkable social legislation such as factory laws, accident insurance for workers, and the limitation of working hours for women and children—as well as many other social reforms considered far too "progressive" at the time in most other industrialized nations.

The progressive political movement started in the U.S. after the Civil War, when Scandinavian farmers began organizing and joining together with other American farmers in Farmers Alliances, especially in the Midwest, to cope with the economic depression of the 1870s. The first Farmers Alliances were nonpolitical and held meetings to discuss agricultural and economic issues. However, members soon realized that conditions could only be improved by passing legislation on state and national levels.

Although none of the political parties spawned by progressivism, such as the Populist Party of the late 19th century, the Progressive Party of 1912, or the Farmer-Labor Party of the 1920s, have survived, almost all of the original Populist demands, such as a graduated income tax and an eight hour work day, were eventually enacted into law. The progressive movement was especially strong in Minnesota and Wisconsin, where it influenced elections and legislation. The progressive principles so important to 19th-century Swedish immigrants are still thriving in the 1990s, and many Americans continue to work for such issues as expanded workers' rights, universal health insurance, environmental protection, a more equitable school system, and programs for the homeless and unemployed. The contributions of Swedish immigrants—especially the pioneers who helped settle our nation's heartland—remain significant and lasting.

Swedish Americans pose by the toboggan slide in Taylor Falls, Minnesota, in about 1890.

STRANGERS IN A STRANGE LAND

Like many immigrant groups, the Swedes banded together in close-knit communities that kept alive the traditions of the homeland, cushioned them against the shocks of their adopted country, and eased their transition to American habits. American customs—or the lack of them—could be disorienting, though gradually immigrants adjusted. Olaf Olsson, a Swedish-American pastor, probably expressed views shared by many of his compatriots when he sent home this report in 1869:

> People in Sweden look upon the Americans as a crowd of wild men and barbarians. This is an error. True, barbarians are found here, bandits of the first class, but I have already met many Americans, for whom I hold the highest respect as men. Although the real American is in his manner forward and unceremonious, so is he nevertheless pleasant and friendly in his association.
> I have already enjoyed with many an obliging hospitality which has astonished me.

Not all Swedish immigrants felt as warmly toward their new American neighbors, however. For those Swedes who had left their homeland hoping to find a land free of class distinctions, episodes such as the one described by this Swedish girl served as a rude awakening:

The first family where I worked knew perfectly well that I spoke French and German. I heard them mention the fact to a guest at the table—but to them I was not any more interesting an object than any peasant girl who could neither read nor write. They might have known that I must have had some sort of education, for the average immigrant girl does not speak many languages. Our relations were entirely impersonal. I found out how foreigners are regarded by the old-line Americans, and I cannot say that it made me feel any more friendly toward America. I was still of the Old World, and who can blame me?

Sadly, not only domestic servants but workers in all occupations encountered such treatment. Although Swedish immigrants were usually welcomed because they furnished the growing nation with labor and useful skills, many Americans typecast their Swedish neighbors as strictly working-class people unfit for higher stations. Perhaps no Swedish American ever described this relationship as eloquently as Hans Mattson, who wrote in the 1850s:

The religious revival movement inspired many Swedish immigrants to attend outdoor meetings such as this one, held in Eastham, Massachusetts.

The Augustana Synod, formed in Illinois in 1850, quickly became the largest Swedish-American religious sect. The synod's founders posed for this photograph in 1885.

The Americans consider themselves very tolerant, and are, in a way, but in many respects they are very intolerant and prejudiced; but this is owing to the lack of knowledge of other nations. It is true that the immigrant is bidden welcome, and is generally well received, but he is expected to be content with shovelling dirt, chopping wood, carrying water, ploughing the fields, and doing other manual labor, no one disputing his right or fitness for these occupations. But when he begins to compete with the native American for honor and emolument in the higher walks of life, he is often met with coldness mingled with envy. It is exceptional that he is recognized as an equal socially. Children of immigrant parents, although born and brought up here, are often subjected to taunts and sneers by their more fortunate playfellows, even within the walls of the American public school.

Faced with such experiences, it is little wonder that Swedish immigrants often sought refuge in communities composed almost entirely of Swedish Americans. Even those like Pastor Olsson, who received a more cordial reception, clung together to lessen the hurt that followed the immigrants in the New World.

Many early settlements, such as Bishop Hill, were formed by families that had crossed the ocean together, then continued their travels as a unit. This helped to

In Chicago, charity food baskets helped many immigrants through the depression.

soften the trauma of moving because the immediate community remained familiar: The customs and language of the people around them had not changed. But few immigrants could afford to stay solely within the safe confines of their homes or their Swedish-speaking communities. To survive in the New World they had to work for English-speaking employers, deal with American merchants, and otherwise confront an English-speaking world in which important matters were conducted along American lines. It was a difficult transition for many Swedes, no matter how excited they felt about the opportunities now open to them.

New arrivals to America usually sought out fellow Swedes, who provided shelter, financial help, and a sympathetic ear. A pair of Swedish-American brothers, who had settled in Brooklyn, New York, testified to the importance of this form of kinship in their postscript to a letter they sent to their sisters in 1880:

> P.S. (Don't show this to anybody.) Poor Nyberg, he didn't have any money, he almost cried when he came to us. He didn't want to tell Almstedt how things were for him. He bade me from the heart that we should help him, which we did. He was quite starved and one foot hurt him. He cried with joy that he found us; he can now live together with us. We will try to find him work. I am very glad he was able to find his way for

it hurts me to see a countryman cold and hungry. It is a serious matter to come to a foreign land with no money, not knowing the language. Nyberg is happy now.

Swedish-American Church Life

In addition to the assistance offered by established arrivals, Swedish Americans often relied on the sanctuary of the church. On the frontier and also in urban areas, Swedish Americans rushed to establish places of worship. They represented a wide variety of denominations. At the turn of the century in Worcester, Massachusetts, for example, eight Swedish churches represented five denominations—Lutheran, Methodist, Baptist, Congregationalist, and Episcopal. Guaranteed religious freedoms denied them in Sweden, Swedish

According to Swedish custom, St. Lucia's lighted candles illuminated a world plunged in darkness. A 1974 celebration in Brooklyn, New York, reenacts this solemn rite.

73

Americans were able to worship according to their own conscience and beliefs.

In Sweden the Lutheran church was, and remains, the state religion. (Born members of the faith, Swedes could not legally withdraw from Lutheranism until 1951.) When radicals such as Eric Jansson and his followers tried to stress the value of individual religious practice and prayer in the home, they were expelled from the country. But even Swedish Americans who remained Lutherans began to alter their expressions of faith and to balk at the secular character of church leaders in Sweden. Many began to embrace a more conservative and rigid form of Lutheranism guided by the powerful Augustana Synod. Originally created in Andover, Illinois, in 1850, the synod quickly became the largest religious sect among Swedish Americans. The Illinois church founded a "conference" or union in 1853, and in 1858 Minnesota's churches followed suit. Between 1860 and 1890 the Augustana Synod grew from 3,000 members—or communicants—to more than 84,000.

Other denominations also found adherents among Swedish Americans, many of whom converted to Methodism, Baptism, and Mormonism. The Swedish Methodist church was the only religious organization that welcomed Swedish immigrants when they came to New York City in the late 1840s and early 1850s. At the same time, many Swedish Methodist congregations sprang up in the East and the Midwest. The Baptists were led

Members of Seattle's Order of Vasa celebrate the Tulip Festival in 1924.

by a former schoolteacher from Gustavsberg, Sweden, Gustav Palmquist, who first converted to Methodism in his homeland and then traveled to America to spread the word. Shortly afterward, he switched to Baptism and founded America's first Swedish Baptist congregation in Rock Island, Illinois, in 1852. Of the Swedish Americans who became Mormons, most had been converted by missionaries in Sweden. Between 1850 and 1909, more than 17,000 Swedes joined that faith, and almost 8,000 of them then came to the United States.

Another sect that gained followers in the Swedish-American community was the Mission Covenant church. Its origins were in the Midwest, but in the 1870s it united with other mission societies to form a national organization, the Evangelical Lutheran Mission Synod. A contemporary missionary organization was the Asgar Synod. When these two groups merged in 1885, they formed the Swedish Evangelical Mission Covenant of America, the second-largest Swedish-American denomination after the Augustana Synod. By 1930 the Swedish Evangelical church included more than 40,000 members.

Apart from their Christian beliefs, the many Swedish-American religious movements shared one essential quality: Their activities extended beyond a purely spir-

In 1961, these citizens of Lindsborg, Kansas, donned native dress as part of the Svensk-Hyllnings Festival.

Before antiforeign hysteria gripped the United States during World War I, Swedish-language newspapers enjoyed large circulations.

itual domain. The effort to unite and benefit the growing community of Swedish Americans spilled over into areas of general public concern, such as education and medical needs. Churches sponsored schools, colleges, and seminaries, along with hospitals, old-age homes, and orphanages. They also published books and journals, sometimes printed by their own firms, and wrote, printed, and distributed newspapers that disseminated religious and social news. Their concern, in short, was to advance the public good. And although their religious practices varied, these different churches served as touchstones in the lives of Swedish Americans.

In addition to serving as the focus of social life, Swedish-American churches became educational centers. One major institution founded by the Augustana Synod in 1860 was the Augustana College and Theological Seminary in Rock Island, Illinois. Its main purpose was training clergy, but it offered courses in the humanities, the sciences, and business. Several other denominations also founded colleges, including Gustavus Adolphus College in St. Peter, Minnesota; Bethany College in Lindsborg, Kansas; Bethel Institute in St. Paul, Minnesota; North Park College in Chicago, Illinois; and Upsala College in East Orange, New Jersey. Their commitment to higher learning continues today.

In addition to gaining formal education, Swedish Americans found it important to keep an understanding of their traditional culture alive. Preserving the folkways and customs of the old country took on major significance for immigrants, who observed that in the New World practical considerations often outweighed spiritual values. As one 19th-century immigrant wrote to a friend at Christmastime:

> These holidays, which are so much celebrated and so looked forward to by the young people in Sweden, are not much observed in America and are celebrated almost alone by Scandinavians and Germans. So if Christmas or New Year's Day comes on a weekday,

you will see among the Americans that their shops are open the whole day and the miners and loggers go to work as usual, and the only change in their diet is a turkey and a drink of liquor.

Such episodes caused many Swedish Americans to feel a rekindled devotion to the habits and customs of their ancestral land. One important means of keeping traditions alive was to celebrate holidays—especially Christmas—according to Swedish custom. The Swedish Christmas season lasted 20 days, beginning with St. Lucia's Day on December 13 and celebrated by a custom still observed in many Swedish-American homes. At dawn, a daughter in the family became St. Lucia. Clothed in a white gown, her head crowned with a wreath of lighted candles, St. Lucy went from room to room, singing traditional songs and serving fresh coffee and buns to household members. On this, one of the longest nights of the year, Lucy's candles conveyed the symbolic importance of light returning to a dark

By the early 1900s, Minneapolis's Swedish-American population had grown large enough to support a Swedish hospital of nursing.

world. The beauty of this ceremony has made it popular outside Sweden, and many contemporary Swedish-American communities continue to await St. Lucy's arrival in the cold December dawn.

The highlight of the holiday was Christmas Eve. A traditional dinner included *lutfisk* (codfish soaked in lye) and rice porridge. Later, *Jultomten*—the Swedish Santa—came with his presents, to the children's delight. Christmas Day was given over to quiet reflection, with an early-morning trip to church for a Christmas service, the *Julotta*, which ended at dawn. December 26 was also a festive day in Sweden; on this day people visited neighbors.

Although Swedish Americans necessarily abbreviated these celebrations, most continued them in some form. "Here it is beginning to get like Sweden," wrote an immigrant in Texas in 1896, "at least at Christmastime, for there is both lutfisk and Christmas porridge, besides a lot of other good things."

Swedish Americans also used the written word to sustain their cultural ties. From the outset of immigration, Swedish newspapers had played an important role by publishing lavish letters of praise from newly settled immigrants. Later, Swedish-American newspapers were equally important in rallying the community and preserving the Swedish language and heritage. In the second half of the 19th century, the years of mass immigration, more than 1,000 different Swedish-Amer-

The study of English was especially important in many Minnesota schools, where the percentage of Swedish Americans was unusually high. This is an English class in St. Paul's Madison School, around 1900.

ican newspapers, in 30 different states, flourished in America. These publications featured the expected news stories, but their advertising and reporting of social, cultural, and political activities also reinforced the national identity of Swedish Americans.

One of the first newspapers of lasting importance was the *Hemlandet* (or *Det Gamla och Det Nya Hemlandet, the Old and New Homeland*). First published in Galesburg, Illinois, in 1855, its offices later moved to Chicago, which eventually boasted the second largest Swedish population of any city in the world, after Stockholm. Written in Swedish, *Hemlandet* advocated the maintenance of inherited Swedish customs and backed church-sponsored parochial schools that conducted classes in Swedish. Conservative in its outlook, *Hemlandet* opposed immigrant associations that featured theater, dance, and social clubs, activities it considered too frivolous and a poor influence on youths who were already losing touch with their national heritage.

Not everyone shared these views. In 1866 a rival newspaper—the liberal *Svenska Amerikanaren* (*Swedish Americans*)—first appeared as a protest against the conservative *Hemlandet*. *Svenska Amerikanaren* encouraged its readers to participate in mainstream American culture. Its editors declared that Swedish Americans must adapt if they were to succeed in their new land and singled out Swedish church schools for attack, claiming that their pastors usually lacked the education necessary for the classroom.

These publications were balanced by less strident journals dedicated to advancing Swedish-American culture. Bearing fanciful names such as *Valkyrian* (*The Valkyrie*) and *Prärieblomman* (*The Prairie Flower*), they attained great popularity because of their comforting tone. They featured essays on topics of general interest, fiction, and poetry written by Swedish and Swedish-American authors, as well as reproductions of works by Swedish-American artists.

Swedish-American Literature

Whether published in journals such as *Valkyrian* or in books, literature helped bridge the Old World and the New by drawing parallels between Swedish traditions and Swedish-American experiences. Sweden had an ancient and splendid tradition of storytelling, dating back to the early sagas of Viking battles and Nordic gods—among the oldest literatures in the world. America offered fertile ground for a new literature and also an audience eager for the written word. In the early 20th century more than 300 Swedish-American writers were penning poetry, short stories, essays, memoirs, novels, and plays. They furnished important insights into the immigrant experience, but their literary quality was generally inferior, influenced by somewhat dated models.

Homesickness was often a unifying theme of Swedish-American literature, mirroring the immigrants' difficulty in adjusting to a new land with its very different values. One of the most effective renderings of this trauma appears at the end of Signe Ankarfelt's poem "Hemlighten" ("The Secret"):

> Every heart must break in two parts.
> One half they will take on their journey
> but the other miserly they will bury
> like a treasure in some hill at home
> and order memory to brood upon it constantly.
> That is the secret you will learn.
> That is the cross they must always carry.

If this personal literature reflected the innermost thoughts of many Swedish Americans, another kind of poetry gave solace and courage to the settlers by depicting Swedes taking their culture with them as they sallied forth into strange territory. This "poetry of pioneering" asserted the Swedes' importance in the formation of America, an expression of Swedish pride in a country that often failed to appreciate these hard-working newcomers:

. . . the Swede is great not only in battle,
he is also victorious on other fields,
and foremost he stands in education, power, and energy
and clears roads where formerly no roads were found.

Ludwig Holmes, "Till Studenter" ("To Students")

Families often found themselves divided by the language barrier.

The themes of homesickness and pioneering gave birth to an amusing offshoot: the travelogue. Fiction rather than poetry, Swedish-American travelogues usually described the adventures of Swedes returning to their native country after many years in America. A realistic premise underlay such stories. Some Swedes did indeed reemigrate, returning to Sweden because they had achieved enough success to live comfortably in their homeland or because they missed their native soil. In a typical travelogue, the hero comically compared his experiences in Sweden with those in America. The most famous of these humorous tales of "innocents abroad" is Frithiof Colling's *Mister Colesons Sverigeresa* (*Mister Coleson's Trip to Sweden*), published in Minneapolis in 1896 under the pseudonym of Gabriel Carlson. In the

In the late 19th century, bilingualism served the differing needs of Swedish-American shoppers at this Minneapolis grocery.

travelogue, Mr. Coleson, newly arrived from America, sporting a breezy manner and fashionable clothes, causes amazement in everyone he encounters in Sweden. The novel vividly portrays stodginess and snobbery in Swedish society, which reminds Mr. Coleson— and his readers—why he had left in the first place.

The Language of Assimilation

The written word helped link traditional Swedish culture and the new American experience, but the spoken word posed the biggest obstacle to Swedish Americans as they struggled to fit into American society. Because the initial wave of immigrants found it very difficult to learn English in the intimate settings of home, church, and social gathering, many Swedish Americans—especially those born in the old country—clung to their native language. Even in the late 1800s, a nucleus of the Swedish-American community still spoke only Swedish.

The "language question" was related to the crucial concept of ethnic identity. Should Swedish Americans become more Americanized, better equipped to succeed in their adopted homeland? Or should they persist in touting their ancestral roots? The issue was much discussed, debated, and written about, and led to a heated dispute between the two most powerful Swedish-American newspapers of the 1860s and 1870s, the conservative *Hemlandet* and the liberal *Svenska Amerikanaren*. Supporting the position of the Augustana Synod, *Hemlandet* asserted that Swedish-American children should attend Swedish-speaking parochial schools and that church services should remain solely in Swedish. *Svenska Amerikanaren* argued that parochial schools held back Swedish-American children by refusing to teach them English.

Loosely linked to the language question were Swedish-American education policies, for it was within the public schools that Swedish children became Americanized. Most Swedish immigrants viewed the free public schools of America as a wonderful advantage. In most other countries, education was a luxury rather than a guaranteed right. In time most Swedish immigrants adjusted to free education, sending their children to public schools whose programs included more than the three Rs ("reading, writing, and 'rithmetic"). Parents were delighted to see their children onstage in school plays or competing in spelling bees in the evenings, when lanterns transformed a one-room schoolhouse into a small theater.

Mister Coleson's Trip to Sweden, *published in 1896, remains the most famous Swedish-American travelogue. Here the hero, dressed to the nines, returns to his native soil.*

This family typifies the level of assimilation most Swedish Americans had attained by World War II.

As the nation became more settled, public schools grew too, not only in size but also in influence. Inside the classroom students used only English; often they were discouraged from speaking Swedish at recess and sometimes penalized for it. This strict approach helped promote the English language but did little to foster ethnic pride among young Swedish Americans.

Because parents longed to assist their children's success in the New World, they worked hard to speak English at home. It was not a quick and easy process, however. English was used more widely at places of business, at school, and when dealing with public officials. But a study of Minneapolis school children as late as 1917–18 found that in households with Swedish-born parents, only 33 percent of the families spoke English at home. The figure soared to 83 percent among those children whose parents had been in America more than 30 years.

This shift in language could breed generational strife. In many families, grandparents and at least one parent continued to speak only Swedish, but their children and grandchildren, even when bilingual, increasingly depended on English. This difference had wider implications: The elderly felt the young ignored their heritage, and the young bridled at the conservatism of their older kin. Gradually, as English became more widely spoken, the conflict was settled.

The language question ended with World War I when Swedish Americans feared being mistaken for foreigners sympathetic to the cause of the German enemy, whose language was related to Swedish. Legislation introduced during the war discouraged all immigrants from speaking or writing in their native tongues. In Iowa speaking one's native language in public was forbidden, and in Minnesota all foreign-language newspapers had to submit translations of any articles that dealt with foreign policy. By the 1920s and 1930s, English had become the primary language of Swedish Americans both inside and outside the home.

One unfortunate result of this adjustment was that the very Swedish-American newspapers that had long advocated English fell victim to their own zeal. By the 1920s a large percentage of the Swedish-American community was composed of second- and third-generation Swedes who spoke only English. These Swedish-Americans felt more American than Swedish and saw no need for a Swedish-American press. Circulation, reduced by the war, plummeted drastically in the next decade. By 1930 the number of Swedish-American newspapers had dwindled to 43; more failed during the Great Depression. Today only seven Swedish-American newspapers remain in print, tenuously linking the Old World and the New.

The language question also divided the Swedish Lutheran church. One reason Lutheranism had originally gained ascendance in 16th-century Sweden was because it held that God's Word should be preached in the language spoken by the common people. In America, however, church leaders had refused to recognize the wisdom of that doctrine and resisted the change from

Swedish to English. Finally, in 1918, when American fears of German sympathizers had reached their highest pitch, the Augustana Synod issued a statement conceding that

> In all our school activities—as well as in all other branches of our church work—it is incumbent upon us to meet existing linguistic needs. Our immigrants and our children must learn the English, the official language of the country, but the Swedish should also be retained as a valuable cultural heritage, as far as possible. The Synod is of the opinion that limitation in the study of foreign languages is a lowering of national education ideals, and that the prohibition of the use of other languages than the English is at variance with American principles of liberty for which the nation has bled and is bleeding.

Some members of the church continued to voice their reluctance, but over the years English won out. In 1924 the synod's general assembly printed its minutes in English for the first time, and by 1925 services were delivered in English. Within a decade, the official language in all American Lutheran churches was English. This shift allowed the church to increase its following, until by 1960 the Augustana Synod included nearly 500,000 members. Two years later, it merged with the United Lutheran Synod (of German origin) and two others to create the Lutheran Church of America, the largest organization of Lutheran churches in the United States. The assimilation of the Swedish church was complete.

A last concession to the English-speaking culture occurred when Swedish Americans slowly began to Americanize their names. Some had done so even in colonial times. John Morton, for example, a signer of the Declaration of Independence, had changed his name from Mortenson. But well into the 19th century, Swedes living in Scandinavian communities did not change their names. Only when second-, third-, and

fourth-generation Swedish Americans moved away from their birthplaces were many names Americanized. Esbjörn became Osborn; Sjöstrand, Seashore; Svenson, Swanson; Bengtson, Benson; Nilsson, Nelson; Hakanson, Hawkinson.

Like virtually every American ethnic group, Swedish Americans have recently begun to question the value of complete assimilation. As they merge closer to the American mainstream, Swedish Americans feel their unique cultural heritage ebbing away. In response, the Swedish Cultural Society of America has come into existence. With chapters in at least six cities, this society has dedicated itself to preserving Swedish culture in America. Similar societies are the American Swedish Historical Foundation in Philadelphia and the Swedish Pioneer Historical Society, founded to conduct research on the Swedes in America. Such organizations encourage Swedish Americans to look beyond their assimilation and remember the heritage of their grandparents and great-grandparents, as well as more distant ancestors who undertook the journey to the New World. ✎

Few traces of the Old World appear in this 1921 gathering of Philadelphia's Americans of Swedish Lineage.

FAMOUS SWEDISH AMERICANS

As a group, the Swedish-American pioneers who settled the Midwest and the Pacific Northwest made the largest impact on their adopted land. But many others, including the handful profiled here, have enriched America's history and culture.

Politics

In 1953, Earl Warren, a Scandinavian American (half Swedish and half Norwegian), was sworn in as chief justice of the United States. Before he retired in 1969, Warren presided over a number of landmark cases, none more important than *Brown v. the Board of Education* (1954), in which the court unanimously ruled that racial segregation of the nation's public schools was unconstitutional.

Warren's mother, Crystal Hernlund Warren, emigrated from Sweden as a very small girl and grew up in Minnesota. There she met her Norwegian-born husband, who eventually became a master car builder for the Southern Pacific Railroad in Los Angeles, California. Their son Earl was born in 1891 and received a law degree in 1912 from the University of California Law School. After serving as the district attorney for Ala-

Congressman John Anderson ran as a third-party candidate in the 1980 presidential race.

meda County, he became the state's attorney general, then its governor. In 1950 Warren gained the office for an unprecedented third term, between two unsuccessful attempts—in 1948 and 1952—to capture the Republican presidential nomination. The man who defeated him in 1952, President Dwight D. Eisenhower, appointed Warren to the highest nonelected office in the country, chief justice of the Supreme Court, a year later. He soon put his stamp on the Court as a dedicated defender of social progress and justice. Earl Warren expressed his own pioneer sentiments when he remarked that "In government, as in all other affairs of life, it is not so much the size of the steps that determine progress as it is the directions in which the steps are taken."

Another Swedish American who failed to win the presidency but nonetheless has had a significant impact on politics in America is John Bayard Anderson. He was born in 1922, the son of E. Albin Anderson, a Swedish immigrant who operated a grocery store in the largely Swedish-American community of Rockford, Illinois. After receiving a law degree from Harvard University, John Anderson practiced law in Rockford and in 1956 won election as the state's attorney for Winnebago County. Four years later, with the overwhelming support of the region's populous and traditionally Republican Swedish-American community, Anderson entered the House of Representatives, elected to serve the Sixteenth Congressional District of Illinois. During the next 20 years, he consistently confounded political analysts by voting liberally on most social welfare issues but conservatively on economic issues. In 1978, Americans for Democratic Action, a liberal lobbying organization, gave Anderson a 55 percent approval rating, rare for a Republican. After losing his party's presidential nomination to Ronald Reagan in 1980, Anderson ran for the office as a third-party candidate appealing to moderate Republicans and also to Democrats. He garnered seven percent of the popular vote.

In 1927, Charles Lindbergh made the first solo air flight across the Atlantic Ocean.

The Dream of Flight

Thousands of years ago the Vikings sailed their ships into the unknown, prepared for peril. Their taste for adventure resurfaced in the legendary aviator Charles Lindbergh. On May 20, 1927, Lindbergh's small Ryan monoplane took off from Roosevelt Field, Long Island, New York, cheered by a group of curious spectators and friends who feared they might be seeing "Slim" for the last time. The *Spirit of St. Louis* skimmed over the treetops and began a transatlantic flight to Paris. To reduce the weight and leave more room for gasoline, Lindbergh brought neither a parachute nor a radio; he carried only five sandwiches and a quart of water. Thirty-three and a third hours later, the 25–year-old Lindbergh became the first solo pilot to guide an airplane across the Atlantic Ocean. When he landed at Paris's Le Bourget airport on May 22, thousands of people were waiting. He stepped out of his small plane and into the realm of legend.

In 1961, Dr. Glenn Seaborg, who discovered plutonium 239, was named by President John F. Kennedy to head the Atomic Energy Commission.

Born in 1902, Lindbergh was the son of an immigrant politician and the grandson of a member of Sweden's parliament. Charles Lindbergh began his flying days as a pilot, wingwalker, and parachutist performing at county and state fairs until 1924, when he entered the U.S. Army flying school in San Antonio, Texas. Following his army stint he flew as an airmail pilot, a treacherous job because of frequent bad weather and primitive communications equipment. All this trained him for his ultimate flight. Today he remains one of America's authentic heroes—the tall, thin Swedish-American boy who changed aviation history.

Scientists

In the 19th century a number of important scientists emigrated to America. One was Gustavus August Eisen, botanist, zoologist, archaeologist, and horticulturist. Born in Stockholm in 1847, Eisen received his Ph.D. from Sweden's Uppsala University in 1873. Later that year he emigrated to America, becoming a citizen in 1887. In the scientific world he is esteemed for his studies of oligochaeta (earthworms), of the blood of batrachians and people, and of the cells of carcinoma. Outside the scientific community, Eisen is best known for founding California's Sequoia National Park in 1890. His other interests included ancient and antique glass, and he helped amass the collections housed in the Freer Gallery of Art of the Smithsonian Institute in Washington, D.C.

Another American scientist of Swedish descent, Glenn Seaborg, won the Nobel Prize in chemistry in 1951 for his work with uranium and plutonium isotopes. Seaborg was born in 1912 to a second-generation Swedish-American father and a Swedish emigrant mother. He earned a Ph.D. in nuclear chemistry from the University of California at Berkeley, then began working there as a research assistant for one of his former professors. After three years of research, Seaborg announced the discovery of a new element, plutonium (atomic number 94), which was heavier than uranium (atomic number 92), regarded at the time as the heaviest element. By 1941 Seaborg had used a cyclotron to prepare and identify a fissionable isotope of this new element: plutonium 239. His discovery and methods greatly increased the world's nuclear fuel potential.

In 1961 Seaborg left the faculty of Berkeley to serve under President John F. Kennedy as head of the Atomic Energy Commission. The first scientist to fill that post, he maintained a moderate stance, struggling, as he put it, "to ride two horses . . . to continue negotiations with the Russians . . . and at the same time keep our defenses strong." Seaborg continued to head the Atomic Energy Commission until 1971.

Business People

Perhaps no American has ever had a greater impact on the way Americans dine than Carl A. Swanson, whose company—C. A. Swanson and Sons—invented TV dinners. Born in Sweden in 1879, Swanson arrived in America at the age of 16. Almost penniless and unable to speak English, he subsisted at first through farm work and menial chores. While employed as a delivery wagon driver, Swanson was befriended by John Jerpe, a fellow Swedish American who owned a food-distribution business. In 1899 the two became partners. Thirty years later, after Jerpe's death, Swanson acquired sole ownership of the company, which he renamed C. A. Swanson and Sons. During World War II, Swanson manufactured canned turkey and other poultry products so successfully that he was known as America's "Turkey King." Under Swanson's leadership, the small company grew, employing more than 3,000 people by the time of his death in 1949. His sons then took over and in the 1950s introduced Swanson's frozen TV dinners.

Another Swedish immigrant who triumphed in the business world was Walter Hoving, formerly the chairman of the board of Tiffany & Company, the world's best-known jewelry store, and president of Lord & Taylor, an elegant clothing retailer. Hoving was born in

Businessman Walter Hoving served as president of the United Service Organizations (USO) during World War II.

Stockholm in 1897 to a prominent physician and a retired diva who had performed with the Swedish Royal Opera. Brought to the United States at the age of six, Hoving later scaled the classic ladder of success in American business: joining a company, making his mark, and then moving on to a higher position in another company. He joined R.H. Macy's & Company as a merchandiser in 1924. Within three years he was promoted to vice-president. He later served as vice-president and chairman of the board at Lord & Taylor before moving to Tiffany's.

His son, Thomas Hoving, has also made his mark in the United States. He became one of the American art scene's most authoritative and controversial figures, serving as director of New York's Metropolitan Museum of Modern Art from 1969 to 1977. Hoving is credited with reinventing the staid and stuffy institution as a vibrant and exciting celebration of art. He installed electronic media for lectures and new lighting for the galleries, hosted concerts and other events, waged massive publicity campaigns, and even slashed admission prices to get the public excited about visiting his museum. Although his methods and philosophy raised many eyebrows, almost every gallery followed the Met's example. Thomas Hoving is also known as an author and as publisher and editor-in-chief of *Connoisseur* magazine.

On the opposite front of American business stood Joel Emanuel Häglund (1879–1915), a Swedish immigrant remembered as one of America's most famous union activists. It is not by the name of Häglund that he is known, however, but as Joe Hill. Hill came to the United States in 1902 and worked at odd jobs. In 1910 he joined the San Pedro, California, chapter of the Industrial Workers of the World (IWW), a labor union that battled unjust bosses. During the following year, while working on the docks, he wrote his first song, "Casey Jones—the Union Scab," in support of striking workers at the South Pacific Railroad. He

Carl Sandburg, one of America's most beloved poets, discovered his ethnic roots late in life.

continued to write protest songs and supported such causes as increased women's membership in the IWW. After Hill suggested the formation of the Workers Moratorium League of New York, it came into being as the IWW Unemployed League.

In 1914 Hill was convicted of murdering a grocer in Salt Lake City. It is widely believed that he was framed by those who feared he represented a threat to company owners and their supporters in government. On November 19, 1915, the state of Utah executed Joe Hill in spite of an international defense movement on his behalf and two pleas made by President Woodrow Wilson to Utah governor William Spry. At his funeral procession in Chicago, 30,000 mourners, sympathizers, and protesters marched. His name lives on in the song "Joe Hill," a folk standard commonly performed by more recent protest singers, such as Joan Baez, who gave a memorable rendition of it in 1969 at the Woodstock Festival.

Writers and Artists

One of the most famous of all Swedish Americans is poet Carl Sandburg. Born in 1878 to Swedish immigrant August Danielson and his wife Clara, Sandburg grew up in Illinois and spent his youth on the road. He was a milk driver, bootblack, soldier (in the Spanish-

American War), hobo, farmer, salesman, and journalist before turning to his true calling: poetry. His popular verse often celebrates the accomplishments and courage of ordinary men and women and made him the most beloved American poet of the 20th century. The first two volumes of his biography of Abraham Lincoln were jointly published in 1926 as *The Prairie Years*. The four-volume sequel, *The War Years*, was awarded the Pulitzer Prize for history in 1940. For many years uninterested in his Swedish heritage, Sandburg later grew proud of it. In 1948 he was a speaker at the Swedish Pioneer Centennial, along with President Harry S. Truman and Prince Bertil of Sweden.

A contemporary of Sandburg's was Carl Milles, whose sculpture pays homage to the natural world, reflecting a Scandinavian love of the outdoors. Especially fascinated with running water, Milles designed many majestic fountains in both Sweden and America.

Carl Milles's fountain, The Meeting of the Waters, *celebrates the convergence of the Mississippi and Missouri rivers.*

Milles's work combines both the power of nature with the mystery of mythology and folklore. He first

visited America in 1929, after two American architects admired his *Diana Fountain* in Stockholm and ordered a copy for Chicago's Michigan Square Building. Milles then emigrated to the United States, settling near Detroit, and established the Cranbrook Academy of Art, where many of his works still can be seen. The first sculpture he created at Cranbrook was the *Jonah Fountain*, which depicts the famous biblical figure stepping out of the mouth of his captor whale. In 1938 Milles completed one of his best-known works, the *New Sweden Monument*, in Wilmington, Delaware. A pillar topped by the sailing ship *Kalmar Nyckel*, the commemorative statue sits near the place where the first Swedish colonists came ashore in 1638. Milles's other works include the gigantic *Meeting of the Waters*, a fountain situated in St. Louis, Missouri, where it celebrates the convergence of the Mississippi and Missouri rivers. Surrounded by tritons and water sprites, its central figure is a 12-foot male figure riding on the back of a dolphin to meet his bride and her escort of sea nymphs.

Despite Milles's lifelong frailty and weakening eyesight, his output was prolific, and he continued working

The "Great Garbo" starred opposite John Barrymore in the 1932 classic Grand Hotel.

until eight months before his death in 1955. His influence was felt most noticeably at the 1939 World's Fair, which featured many sculptures based on his work. His final piece, *St. Martin of Tours*, was dedicated at the new cultural center in Kansas City, Missouri, in 1958. This sculpture depicts the saint's most famous act, sharing his cloak with a beggar. It is a fitting conclusion to Milles's generous career.

Entertainers

"I want to be alone," said Greta Garbo in the 1932 film *Grand Hotel*. This remark, now enshrined in movie lore, accurately describes the woman dubbed by early Hollywood's publicity agents as the "Mysterious Stranger" and the "Swedish Sphinx." Born in 1905 in Stockholm as Greta Louis Gustafson, she grew up in poverty and went to work at the age of 14, immediately after her father's death. She was employed first in a barbershop, lathering the faces of men waiting to be shaved. Next she became a salesgirl in a department store. It was there that the pretty young woman was asked to act in a short publicity film, *How Not to Dress* (1921). More film assignments soon followed, and, encouraged by her success, she applied for and won a scholarship to the royal dramatic training school.

While enrolled there, she caught the eye of film director Mauritz Stiller, a Russian-Jewish immigrant who was one of Sweden's "golden age" directors. He cast her in *Gösta Berlling's Saga*, and Garbo's sensational career was launched. Before long Stiller was invited to Hollywood, and he insisted that his protégé accompany him. Stiller fared poorly in America and eventually returned to Sweden, but Garbo stayed on and became perhaps the greatest of all film stars. Her most famous films include *Flesh and the Devil* (1927), *Anna Christie* (1930, based on the play by Eugene O'Neill), *Anna Karenina* (1935), *Camille* (1936),

The many talents of Ann-Margret have made her a top name in films, on stage, and on television.

and *Ninotchka* (1939). Some critics claim, however, that her finest roles are those she played in her earlier, Swedish films.

Garbo's acting career ended in 1941 with her last movie, *Two-Faced Woman*. She spent the next 55 years dividing her time between her homes in Switzerland, the Riviera, and New York City, dodging all photographers and refusing all interviews. In spite of the secrecy and her desire to be left alone (or maybe because of it), Garbo became even more of a mysterious screen goddess to her movie fans. As screen scholar Robert Osbourne, a columnist for the *Hollywood Reporter*, once said of this actress who had become the quintessential Hollywood star, "Her silence preserved the magic that made her so fascinating. Maybe if we knew what really went on inside her, she would not have appeared half as interesting."

The "Swedish Sphinx" died on Easter Sunday, April 15, 1990, at the age of 84. Later that year, fans paid over $20.7 million for 270 pieces of furniture and personal belongings from her estate that were auctioned off at Sotheby's in New York City. (One perfume bottle alone went for $18,700.) Even after her death, Garbo's fans were still seeking a piece of the legend.

Another great Swedish-American actress was Ingrid Bergman. Born in Stockholm in 1915, she was raised by relatives after her parents died. She graduated from high school, joined the Royal Dramatic Theatre, and within a year had landed leading roles in Swedish films. By 1936 she had so impressed the Hollywood mogul David O. Selznick that he brought her to America. In the next decade Bergman starred in such memorable movies as *Casablanca* (1942), *Gaslight* (an Oscar-winning performance in 1944), and *Notorious* (1946). Her wholesome beauty and thoughtful characterizations delighted critics as well as the public, although her popularity suffered in the 1950s after a highly publicized romance with the renowned Italian film director Roberto Rossellini. Denounced on the

The comic repartee between ventriloquist Edgar Bergen and his puppet Charlie McCarthy delighted radio audiences in the 1940s.

After inventing xerography in 1938, Chester Carlson founded the Xerox Corporation.

floor of Congress and reviled by conservative women's clubs and religious groups, Bergman left the United States and pursued her career overseas. Gradually, however, her American fans wooed her back, and she appeared in films, on stage, and on television. She died in 1982.

A more recent star is Ann-Margret, who began her career as a singer and dancer, then became one of her generation's best-known movie, television, and night-club performers. She was born Ann-Margret Olsson in 1941 in the Swedish village of Valsjoby. At five she came to America. As a very young girl, she began singing and dancing at church socials, weddings, and private parties.

In 1960, when she was singing in a hotel lounge, the comedian George Burns heard her and booked her as his opening act in Las Vegas. Within three years she had become the new face in Hollywood, starring opposite Pat Boone in *State Fair*, Bette Davis in *A Pocketful of Miracles*, and Dick Van Dyke in *Bye Bye Birdie*. For the next 10 years Ann-Margret struggled to overcome her stereotyped image as a Hollywood sex symbol, finally breaking through in 1971 with a serious role in *Carnal Knowledge*, costarring with a fellow Swedish American, Candice Bergen. Recognized as a serious and talented actress, Ann-Margret expanded her range with roles in *Tommy*, *Magic*, and the television movie *The Two Mrs. Grenvilles*. After making 42 motion pictures, Ann-Margret is the winner of five Golden Globe Awards and has been nominated for two Oscars and four Emmys—in addition to maintaining a career as a live performer around the world.

Although Swedes are generally admired for their sense of purpose, their no-nonsense approach to life, one Swedish American's gift for comedy and entertainment brought him the love of millions of fans. This was ventriloquist Edgar Bergen, beloved creator of the wooden puppet Charlie McCarthy, a wisecracking fellow who is now part of the Smithsonian Institute's entertainment collection. Bergen was born in 1903 to Swedish parents in Chicago. He began his career as a ventriloquist and magician during the summers of 1922–25. Fame arrived after his first radio appearance on December 17, 1936. The jokes Bergen traded with Charlie—and also with puppets Mortimer Snerd and Effie Klinker—brought laughter to homes all across America.

Bergen and his wife, Nellie, had one daughter, Candice Bergen, who has achieved acclaim in her own right. After a career as a model and a photojournalist, Candice Bergen started acting and was applauded for her roles in films such as *The Group* and *Carnal Knowledge*. In 1987, she premiered as the star of a long-running television comedy called *Murphy Brown*, for which she has won five Emmy awards, the most ever by a lead actor or actress in the same series.

These Swedish Americans have won more fame than their fellow immigrants, but they are not alone in blazing pioneer trails that have benefited and inspired other Americans.

CONCLUSION

Considering the great number of Swedes who immigrated to America between 1851 and 1930, it may seem surprising that Swedish emigration has now virtually ceased. There are reason for the decline. The conditions that once chased Swedes from their homeland—unemployment, overpopulation, the shortage of arable farmland, religious repression—scarcely exist any longer. The same can be said of the unique attractions—especially the enormous tracts of affordable land—that America once offered immigrants. From 1931 to 1970, only about 50,000 Swedes entered the United States—an average slightly exceeding 1,000 per year. From 1971 to the present, the numbers have dwindled even further.

The 4 million Swedish Americans who inhabit our nation today have greatly enriched the lives of all Americans and will undoubtedly continue to do so. An unbroken line of achievement links the first Swedish colonists who introduced log cabins to the new land—to the current wave of scientists, inventors, politicians, professionals, and artists.

No Swedish-American contribution, however, rivals that of the pioneers who settled the unclaimed territories that stretched westward from America's colonial communities. Before the great waves of Swedish immigrants began arriving in America in the 1850s and 1860s, states such as Illinois, Nebraska, and Kansas were unpopulated prairies. Similarly, regions to the north—Minnesota, Wisconsin, the Dakotas, and the Canadian provinces of Manitoba and Saskatchewan—were mostly forested regions with few American settlements. And farther westward, the dense woodlands of the Pacific Northwest—Washington, Alaska, British Columbia—remained almost totally unpopulated. Helped by other immigrants, especially those from Norway and Germany, Swedish Americans tamed the frontier. Within 50 years homes and farms had sprung up, then entire towns and cities. Swedish Americans led the way, felling trees, busting sod, farming the land, and establishing communities. When they had finished, American and Canadian communities stretched all the way to the Pacific Ocean.

Although Swedish immigrants were looked down upon and even exploited by other Americans when they first arrived, they quickly proved to be very capable of participating in a representative form of self-government. After all, the Riksdag had been inspired by the principles of the U.S. Constitution, and Swedish immigrants, most of whom were literate, were already well aware of the role government could play in promoting social reform and equal economic opportunity. Their Protestant faith also made them more acceptable to many of their new neighbors.

With each succeeding generation, barriers of language and culture melted away, and Swedish Americans triumphantly entered many fields. The children of farmers, loggers, and miners became executives, research scientists, senators, congressional representatives, and even a Supreme Court justice. Swedish Americans have truly become an integral part of American society.

Today's immigrants from Sweden no longer face the great cultural obstacles that daunted their forebears. Many contemporary Swedish immigrants can speak English before they arrive in America, partly because they belong to the educated, upper echelons of Swedish society. Instead of clearing land or laboring in the mines or on the railroads, they work as professionals, executives, and artisans. They win acceptance more quickly than did their second-, third-, and fourth-generation compatriots. But these newcomers share the same aspirations as the poor farmers who risked everything more than a century ago. Like them, and like all American's immigrants, they long to gain a valued place in their adopted homeland.

Many Swedish Americans still incorporate some touches of their Swedish cultural heritage. Swedish bakeries like those in Brooklyn, New York, still make *limpa*, a delicious rye bread; some Lutheran churches, like the one in Woodstock, Connecticut, still occasionally conduct services in Swedish; and throughout the country, many Swedish-American families gather for smorgasbord on Christmas Eve. Over half say that they stay in touch with relatives still in Sweden, and over a third travel to their ancestral homeland. Like so many of their neighbors, Swedish immigrants and their offspring know that being American does not mean giving up cherished cultural practices.

Swedish Americans in New York City perform the Vävavadmal, an ancestral dance.

FURTHER READING

Ander, O. Fritiof. *The Cultural Heritage of the Swedish Immigrant.* New York: Arno Press, 1956.

Benson, Adolph B., and Naboth Hedin. *Americans from Sweden.* New York: Lippincott, 1950.

Benson, Adolph B., and Naboth Hedin, eds. *Swedes in America, 1638–1938.* New Haven, CT: Yale University Press, 1938.

Bjorn, Thyra Ferre. *Papa's Wife.* New York: Holt, Rinehart and Winston, 1956.

Hasselmo, Nils. *Swedish America, an Introduction.* Minneapolis, MN: Brings Press, 1976.

Kastrup, Allan. *The Swedish Heritage in America.* St. Paul, MN: North Central Publishing Company for the Swedish Council of America, 1975.

Ljungmark, Lars. *Swedish Exodus.* Trans. Kermit B. Westerberg. Carbondale and Edwardsville, IL: Southern Illinois University Press for the Swedish Pioneer Historical Society, 1979.

Moberg, Vilhelm. *The Emigrants.* Trans. Gustaf Lannestock. London: Max Reinhardt, 1956.

Sandburg, Carl. *Always the Young Strangers.* New York: Harcourt and Brace, 1953.

INDEX

Picture Credits

We would like to thank the following sources for providing photographs: Acme Photo: p. 94; American Swedish Historical Museum: pp. 26, 34; The Bettmann Archive: pp. 13, 18, 20, 22, 23, 24, 29, 37, 48; Bishop Hill Heritage Association: pp. 38, 44, 49, 50(top), 51(top), 56; Fritjof Collins: p. 83; Giraudon/Art Resource: p. 17; Johannes Hoving Collection, Balch Institute Library, Philadelphia, PA, Photo Group 25: p. 87; Hubert Josse/Art Resource: p. 27; The Kansas State Historical Society; Topeka: p. 75; Katrina Thomas: pp. 73, 105; Library of Congress: pp. 28, 30, 32, 36, 39, 40, 41, 52(bottom), 53, 54–55, 57, 58–59, 60, 62, 70, 76, 84, 88; The Metropolitan Museum of Art, George A. Hearn Fund, 1942: pp. 50-51 (bottom); Minnesota Historical Society: pp. 42, 47, 68-69, 77, 78, 82; Missouri Historical Society: p. 97; National Portrait Gallery, Smithsonian Institution, Washington, D.C.: p. 91; New York Public Library: p. 43; Norwegian National Tourist Office: p. 19; SEF/Art Resource: p. 21; Smithsonian Institution, Washington, D.C.: p. 52 (top); Special Collections Division, University of Washington Libraries: pp. 61, 63, 74; Springer/Bettmann Film Archives: pp. 98, 99; State Historical Society of Wisconsin: p. 81; Mark Stein Studios: p. 25; Swedish American Historical Society, Chicago: pp. 35, 64, 72; Swenson Swedish Immigration Research Center, Augustana College, Rock Island, IL: p. 71; United Press International Photo: pp. 90, 96; UPI/Bettmann Archive: p. 92; UPI/Bettmann Newsphotos: p. 100; Xerox Corporation: p. 101

ALLYSON McGILL, a Swedish American, holds a doctorate in English literature from Indiana University. Her articles on Victorian England and colonial immigrants have appeared in scholarly journals and publications.

SANDRA STOTSKY is director of the Institute on Writing, Reading, and Civic Education at the Harvard Graduate School of Education as well as a research associate there. She is also editor of *Research in the Teaching of English*, a journal sponsored by the National Council of Teachers of English.

Dr. Stotsky holds a bachelor of arts degree with distinction from the University of Michigan and a doctorate in education from the Harvard Graduate School of Education. She has taught on the elementary and high school levels and at Northeastern University, Curry College, and Harvard. Her work in education has ranged from serving on academic advisory boards to developing elementary and secondary curricula as a consultant to the Polish Ministry of Education. She has written numerous scholarly articles, curricular materials, encyclopedia entries, and reviews and is the author or coauthor of three books on education.

REED UEDA is associate professor of history at Tufts University. He graduated summa cum laude with a bachelor of arts degree from UCLA, received master of arts degrees from both the University of Chicago and Harvard University, and received a doctorate in history from Harvard.

Dr. Ueda was research editor of the *Harvard Encyclopedia of American Ethnic Groups* and has served on the board of editors for *American Quarterly, Harvard Educational Review, Journal of Interdisciplinary History*, and *University of Chicago School Review*. He is the author of several books on ethnic studies, including *Postwar Immigrant America: A Social History, Ethnic Groups in History Textbooks*, and *Immigration*.

DANIEL PATRICK MOYNIHAN is the senior United States senator from New York. He is also the only person in American history to serve in the cabinets or subcabinets of four successive presidents—Kennedy, Johnson, Nixon, and Ford. Formerly a professor of government at Harvard University, he has written and edited many books, including *Beyond the Melting Pot, Ethnicity: Theory and Experience* (both with Nathan Glazer), *Loyalties*, and *Family and Nation*.